2nd Edition

HEALING YOUR DEPRESSION

A Catholic Perspective

D1552714

THOMAS SYRE SR, MPH, PH.D.

Foreword by Rev. Fr. Worku Yohannes Gebre, OFMCap, D.Min.

Syre Publications, 2023 © Thomas Syre Sr. (1950-), with a Foreword by Worku Yohannes Gebre.

Bibliographic referencing: Catholicism, depression relief, mental health therapy, positive psychology, mental well-being, happiness.

Select positive psychology activities are derived from an evolving self-help manuscript on depression and anxiety relief by James L. Krag, MD, and Thomas Syre Sr., MPH, Ph.D.

Warm acknowledgments to Rev. Fr. Silvio Kaberia, Rev. Fr. Ritche Sarabia, Rev. Fr. Armando Herrera, Blessed Sacrament Catholic Church; Philip Andrew Mayles, LPC, Harrisonburg-Rockingham Community Services Board; and Mehretu Zeray and Rahel Yosief, Habesha Restaurant. All reside in Harrisonburg, Virginia. A warm acknowledgment is extended to James L. Krag, MD in Charlottesville, Virginia. Editorial help was provided by Jim Gallant in Massanutten, Virginia.

A portion of the Amazon royalties will be donated to Blessed Sacrament's Knights of Columbus Chapter for service support to intellectually and developmentally disabled adults in Harrisonburg.

This paperback is printed and bound in the United States and is also available in Kindle format on Amazon.com.

I dedicate *Healing Your Depression: A Catholic Perspective, 2nd Ed.,* to my daughter and son with great love, pride, and respect.

Table of Contents

Foreword 1

By Rev. Father Worku Yohannes Gebre, OFMCap, D.Min.

Chapter 1 7

Depression Overview and Statistics

Chapter 2 15

Recommendations

Chapter 3 65

Personal Actions

Chapter 4 109

The Therapist Search

Chapter 5 135

Popular Therapeutic Modalities

Chapter 6 169

Journaling

Chapter 7 179

Embrace a Heightened Quality of Life

Life Synopsis of the Author 193

Recent Publications 195

Prayer to St. Dymphna, Patron Saint for Mental Wellness 197

Index 199

Foreword

By Rev. Father Worku Yohannes Gebre, OFMCap, D.Min.

Writing a Foreword for *Healing Your Depression: A Catholic Perspective, 2nd Ed.,* is a pleasure. Syre's second edition adds more information to the field of Catholic writings, the mental health discipline, and positive psychology. This book is a significant addition to the field of self-help paperback, digital, and audio offerings in the American non-fiction marketplace.

Most self-help offerings are secular, but the author has written one with a faith-based view. It contributes to the helping literature on mental health and Catholicism. The Catholic content is written following the teachings of the Catholic Church and the health-related content is current science-based information gleaned from reliable national websites and scholarly publications. The empirical findings shared hold advantages over self-help books that focus on anecdotal personal stories and limited clinical observations.

I have known Dr. Syre for years as a researcher, educator, and friend. He helped me with the final editing of my D.Min. thesis on Catholic school principal practices while I studied at the Catholic Theological Union in Chicago years ago. We remain colleagues in writing projects for Ethiopia's Capuchin Franciscan Institute of Philosophy and Theology in Addis Ababa, Ethiopia.

As you read, you will learn that *Healing Your Depression: A Catholic Perspective, 2nd Ed.,* can help you to enrich your faith while healing from depression. Your faith and actions will aid in your recovery. Embrace your faith and pray for healing because God and his saints are always by your side and hear your prayers.

You learn in your reading that God calls you to do more than pray and actively take part in the Catholic Church and its sacraments. The author shares suggested activities that will lead you to improved mental and physical health.

Relevance to Mental Health

As you read, you learn ways to improve your life. You learn that mental health well-being is brought on by your faith and planned activities that meet your interests, needs, values, and resources. Syre's advice is neither sentimental nor simplistic, and his recommendations include changes in interpersonal, medical, and behavioral practices. He asks you to catalog them by filling in the pages in the later chapters. This self-help book gives you information and activities to enhance your spiritual, physical, and mental health.

As you pursue healing and well-being, know that your body is a temple of the Holy Spirit and intended to be a holy instrument for God's unique usage. In one of the chapters, the author discusses the importance of improving physical health through behavioral change and regular care of your ailments.

The author mentions priestly duties. Recognize that priests provide spiritual counsel inside and outside of the confessional. Make appointments with your parish priest to discuss the problems you face in life. However, when necessary, the author discusses the selection and use of a licensed psychotherapist to help you. He discusses psychiatrists, therapists, and the mental health system in the United States and how to use the system wisely.

You learn about therapeutic modalities to make you a more educated consumer of mental health services. As you read, it is clear how the positive psychology modality and its PERMA Model can help everyone regardless of mental health status.

Writing is therapeutic. Syre discusses how journaling helps you in your journey to wellness. Journaling records your path to well-being, and he discusses its benefits. He provides writing prompts in the journaling chapter.

Each of us is gifted with a calling by God to love and serve. Pursue your calling with daily devotion to the Trinity regardless of your calling to lay or consecrated religious life. The discussion about quality-of-life issues ranging from spiritual to environmental matters is enlightening. The author guides you to improve your life regardless of circumstances or personal resources. Consider his talk about the paths to happiness and the wisdom and advice of Pope Francis and the saints.

Consider the research findings shared by the author and especially the warnings about society's technology dependence and his suggestions for improving interpersonal relationships with family and friends. He responds to the interpersonal disconnection and loneliness epidemic in the United States. Make this book a reading companion you annotate and share with others. Visit the recommended websites, review the suggested books, and read the journal articles mentioned.

As you read *Healing Your Depression: A Catholic Perspective, 2nd Ed.,* pursue a closer personal relationship with the Trinity by reading the *Bible* and the *Catechism of the Catholic Church.* These are found in your church library and on the internet. Add Syre's book to your personal library collection of Catholic readings.

Seek support from people close to you. Rely on your parish priest and friends in your church community. They can give guidance, strength, and comfort. Healing is possible through your faith and actions. And the grace of God.

Practicing Catholics and the Church Precepts

The author discusses the importance of the Catholic faith and church practices in your life. I remind my church parishioners and pre-seminary students at the Institute in Addis Ababa, Ethiopia that being a "practicing" Catholic requires effort. We are asked to follow the church's five precepts in paragraphs 2021 through 2023 of the *Catechism of the Catholic Church.*

The first precept of a practicing Catholic is, "You shall attend Mass on Sundays and holy days of obligation." It requires us to sanctify Sunday and commemorate the Resurrection of the Lord as well as the principal liturgical feasts honoring the mysteries of the Lord, the Blessed Virgin Mary, and the saints.

The second precept is, "You shall confess your sins at least once a year." Confession ensures preparation for the Eucharist by the reception of the Sacrament of Reconciliation. Confession continues Baptism's work of conversion and forgiveness. You are wise to receive the sacrament at least once each month.

The third precept is, "You shall receive the Sacrament of the Eucharist at least once during the Easter season." This Holy Communion guarantees, as a minimum, the reception of the Lord's Body and Blood in connection with the Paschal feasts, the origin and center of the Christian liturgy.

The fourth precept is, "You shall observe the days of fasting and abstinence established by the feasts." Following this precept helps us acquire further mastery over our instincts and freedom of heart.

The fifth and final precept is, "You shall help provide for the material needs of the Church." We, the faithful, are obliged to provide financial aid to the church according to our ability. You can also meet the needs of the church through service to the church.

As a Priest

Religious practices and spirituality profoundly influence our lives. Throughout my life as a Capuchin friar and priest, I have seen in my global travels that happiness has little to do with ownership of modern amenities like automobiles, televisions, laptops, or access to the internet. The author suggests leading a more minimalist life, and I agree.

Aside from life's basics, the essential things in life are not things. We may live in one of the richest or poorest nations in the world, but we can find peace, hope, and happiness through our reverent lives, celebrating our faith, and service to others.

The news broadcasts in the United States report weekly on the tragic and unexpected suicides of celebrities, writers, comedians, and actors. These sad deaths are a reminder that personal material wealth, physical possessions, and fame do not assure happiness or good mental health.

Pope Francis is quoted in the concluding chapter of this book about joy. The pope shares that joy and good mental health require a spiritual value system and faith. In communion with others, I ask that you embrace, live, and practice your Catholic faith and acknowledge its influence on your well-being and happiness. If there is a secret to happiness and good mental well-being, it begins with God and your faith.

The path to healing brings personal renewal. Recovery from depression and other mental illnesses can lead to a new enthusiasm for life. Your efforts to heal are not obstacles to happiness but rather a means to achieve more profound and lasting happiness.

Prayer, the adoration of God, and a deep and personal relationship with our Lord and Savior, Jesus Christ, bring us happiness. Seek Jesus in all persons around you and take part in your Catholic faith practices. These actions will bring you true joy.

In closing, Syre has authored a post-pandemic self-help book to help you enrich your faith, relieve you of your depression, and feel better. His many suggested behavioral and attitudinal changes are ambitious and, to some, may be somewhat overwhelming. But, as you read, embrace the content that will help and guide you and leave the rest. May your Catholic faith be strengthened along with your mental and physical well-being.

Rev. Fr. Worku Yohannes Gebre, OFM Cap, D.Min.
Pastor, Saint Francis Roman Catholic Parish &
Rector, Capuchin Franciscan Institute of Philosophy and Theology
Addis Ababa, Ethiopia

Chapter 1

Depression Overview and Statistics

About Depression

No one is immune from depression. It occurs across races, genders, ages, socioeconomic strata, professions, educational backgrounds, and religious groups. While it often first appears in the teenage years, it can begin at any time in a person's life.

If you are struggling with depression, you are not alone. Depression is one of the most commonly diagnosed mental illnesses in the United States. Historically, five percent of adults in our country have been reported to suffer from this malady. The numbers have increased since 2019 with the advent of the coronavirus pandemic. Depression has become more pronounced in its symptoms among adults, adolescents, and children.

It is not a new illness. Depression existed long before the pandemic. The coronavirus pandemic only worsened the breadth and severity of the problem. The National Institute of Mental Health (NIMH) continues to report in 2023 that depression is one of the leading causes of disability among U.S. citizens aged fifteen to forty-four.

Of those affected by depression, many have depressive symptoms so severe that their illness dramatically reduces their levels of happiness and quality of life and limits what they can and cannot do. For many, it affects their health, activities of daily living, employment, and relationships.

The number of people suffering nationally from depression in 2023 has risen. Nearly one in five adults is experiencing two or more symptoms of depression.

According to the prestigious and reliable Mayo Clinic and National Institute of Mental Health (NIMH), depression is also referred to as "major depressive disorder" or "clinical depression." Mental health researchers and professionals report that it is a severe mood disorder that presents as "major depression," "persistent depressive disorder," "perinatal depression," "seasonal affective disorder," and "depression with symptoms of psychosis." Depression disorders have similar symptoms.

The symptoms of depression consistently reported in mental health literature and found on the Mayo Clinic, U.S. NIMH, and similar reliable websites include:

- Feelings of sadness, tearfulness, emptiness, or hopelessness

- Angry outbursts, irritability, or frustration, even over small matters

- A loss of interest or pleasure in everyday activities, such as hobbies, sports, or sex

- Sleep disturbances, including insomnia or sleeping too much

- Fatigue and lack of energy; even small tasks take extra effort

- Increased food consumption leading to weight gain or reduced appetite and weight loss

- Anxiety, agitation, or restlessness in daily activities

- Slowed thinking, speaking, or body movements

- Feelings of worthlessness or guilt, fixating on past failures or self-blame

- Trouble concentrating, making decisions, and remembering things

- Recurrent thoughts of death, suicide thoughts, suicide attempts, or suicide

It is not known exactly what causes clinical depression, but researchers suggest that certain factors are involved. These factors include inherited traits, as depression is more common among blood relatives. It involves changes in brain chemistry, our neurotransmitters, and hormone imbalances that can result from pregnancy, thyroid problems, menopause, or other medical conditions.

Factors increase the risk of triggering depression in children, adolescents, adults, and older Americans. These risks include:

- Certain personality traits, such as low self-esteem, over-dependence on others, and pessimism

- Traumatic or stress-filled experiences, including emotional, physical, or sexual abuse, the death of a loved one, difficult interpersonal relationships, family conflicts, or financial problems

- Blood relatives with a history of depression, addiction to alcohol or drugs, or bipolar disorder

- Abuse of, or addiction to, alcohol or recreational drugs

- Sexual orientation and being lesbian, gay, bisexual, or transgender

- Serious chronic illnesses including cancer, stroke, heart disease, or chronic pain

- Select prescription medications that treat hypertension, inflammatory diseases, insomnia, seizures, and Parkinson's disease

- Limited access to primary health care, food, or adequate housing

- A lack of family and social support

Declines in mental health were recently brought to the forefront during the pandemic, which saw everyday life severely disrupted for residents in the United States and globally. Quarantines forced social isolation and an abrupt "disconnect" from people, places, and things. These disconnects are now common in our society.

Depression affects people of all ages, genders, races, and sociological and educational backgrounds. As previously mentioned, no one is immune from this mental illness, and few seek care.

If you are reading this book and seeking relief from your depression symptoms, you are in a small minority.

Most people who suffer from depression suffer in silence. Hesitation to seek care involves the continuing stigma of mental illness, an ignorance of how to use the mental health care delivery system, impaired access to medical and mental health care, and a lack of financial resources.

According to the U.S. Centers for Disease Control and Prevention (CDC) and the National Center for Health Statistics (NCHS), in 2019, only nineteen percent of adults needing mental health care received any form of treatment in the past twelve months. Sixteen percent of those receiving care took prescription psychotropic medications for their illness.

Those who suffer from depression know how debilitating it can be. It is a heavy personal and family burden that can torment the person. It clouds judgment, separates people from joy, and isolates depressed persons from loved ones and friends. It diminishes the quality of life regardless of social or economic circumstances.

Healing is Possible

Regardless of the length and severity of the illness, you can heal from depression and reach happiness and well-being. For Catholics, it first involves prayer and active participation in the Catholic Church and its sacraments. Recognize that your faith and Catholic Church are gifts.

Begin your healing journey first by reaching out to your parish priest for counsel, prayer, and the Sacrament of the Anointing of the Sick.

Healing also requires actions, including changing your ways of thinking and your lifestyle and behaviors. Reach out to your medical doctor for a comprehensive physical exam, obtain a definitive depression diagnosis, and explore the best personal treatment options for you. You heal by carefully planned changes in your life.

You also reach out by choosing and seeing an effective therapist if needed. You may receive help from antidepressant medicines for a brief period while in therapy. Outpatient day treatment may help.

Finally, hospitalization may be advisable if you risk harming yourself or another.

Depression can be healed and your life transformed in spirit, body, and mind. It is through the presence of God, your faith, and enthusiastic participation in the Catholic Church and its community, sacraments, and rituals.

Healing is work and involves finding ways to serve the Catholic Church and its parishioners, making and meeting workable goals, receiving proper medical care, initiating psychotherapy if needed, exercising, getting good sleep, and eating correctly. It means engaging in daily prayer life, enhancing your relationships with God and family, and connecting and spending time with people who emotionally support and care about you.

Sources, Lenses, and Applications

Factual and current information from various sources is presented on the following pages. Government sources include the U.S. Centers for Disease Control and Prevention (CDC), the National Institutes of Mental Health (NIMH), the National Center for Health Statistics (NCHS), and the National Library of Medicine (NLM).

Non-governmental internet resources include, for example, the American Psychiatric Association, the American Psychological Association, the National Alliance on Mental Illness, the Anxiety & Depression Association of America, the PubMed search engine, WebMD, and the VIA Character Institute. These resources are easily found on the internet with your preferred browser search engine. The research findings on Google Scholar are also reliable resources.

Sources also include fact-based publications written by scholars and practitioners focusing on mental health and mental illness, and they are referenced. All publications are available either on Amazon.com or the internet for more reading.

Because of its reported success in treating depression, positive psychology is emphasized in this book, and the reader is asked to complete a positive psychology activity at the end of each chapter. These are adapted from the research and clinical practices of Martin Seligman, Ph.D., a psychology professor considered by some the father of positive psychology, and Tayyad Rashid, Ph.D., a clinical psychology professor at the University of Toronto Scarborough, who teaches positive psychology.

As you read, fill in the lines that will solidify your thoughts and track your plans, activities, and progress in improving your well-being.

As a method of journaling, you can include your deeply personal, private, and confidential thoughts on your recovery in your chapter activity writing. Each chapter activity can be completed once or multiple times.

The application of eye lenses is used throughout the book.

These lenses could be considered like a pair of eyeglasses that influence your vision and affect how you see the world. They influence your vision of how exciting and wonderful life is or how frightening and unpredictable it might be. The lenses you choose influence what you see.

The author asks you to look through several different lenses as you read the chapters. These lenses include, for example, faith-based, kindness, compassion, and love lenses. To see a kinder, more compassionate, and loving world, you must choose the lens through which you see. For example, when you view others through a lens of kindness, you are more likely to feel compassion for them rather than judgment or discrimination.

Healing Your Depression: A Catholic Perspective, 2nd Ed., will make you more knowledgeable about depression and its treatment, the mental health care system, therapeutic modalities, community mental health providers, and medicines to treat it. You will become a wiser consumer of mental health services.

Your faith is fundamental in your life. Apply the lens of Christian faith with the discussion of healing from depression. Your Catholic faith and active participation in the church can be integral to your life and make it possible to heal and lead a joy-filled life regardless of circumstances.

Finally, this book is a spiritual, mental, and behavioral resource. The message is straightforward. It asks you to take personal actions and use the mental health care system knowledgeably. With prayer and God's grace, you can heal and live joyfully, and as Pope Francis reminds us in his writings and proclamations, "God wants us to be happy and live joyfully."

Chapter 2

Recommendations

We can live this life to the fullest- with our feet firmly planted on the ground- and respond courageously to whatever challenges come our way.

Pope Francis

Introduction

If you are a practicing Catholic, you are truly blessed. Your faith and active participation in the Catholic Church and its sacraments bring you spiritual gifts. Your faith and courage can sustain you through the tough times and any mental health problems you experience.

Please return if you are a Catholic who has left the Catholic Church and non-practicing. If you have become a Protestant church member, please consider returning to the Catholic Church for the Mass and sacraments. You are warmly welcomed back into the fold.

If you were baptized in the Catholic Church but claim the Catholic faith in name only or attend church only for Ash Wednesday and the Christmas and Easter Masses, become more active in your church. Attend Mass weekly, take part in the Sacrament of Reconciliation at least monthly, and receive the Eucharist weekly. Fast and give what you can to the Catholic Church with your time, service, and money.

Mass attendance improves your mood and makes you a more devoted church member. Attending Mass with friends can bring you camaraderie in Christ. The recitation of prayers can bring you inner peace. Making the sign of the cross, which dates to the second century, is a prayer, a blessing, a sacramental, and a beloved ritual.

Your Catholic Church can become a second home to you. See your local parish priest for monthly confession because secrets keep you sick, and confession cleanses your soul. Sharing and discussing life's challenges with a priest can calm you and bring you guidance and peace.

Consider your parish priest a wise and holy friend and blessed confessor. The parochial vicar and deacons are also decent and reverent religious persons who help with the pastoral care of the parish. These religious people are blessings in your church community.

As you listen to the Mass's first and second readings and then the sermons delivered by the priest or deacon, listen for what you may learn to strengthen your knowledge and faith-based practices. Listen to understand what can make you a better Catholic and improve your faith practices with your family, friends, and society. This is not a time for criticism of the sermon's length or content; it is a time to learn and grow in faith.

Volunteer as an usher, reader, Eucharistic minister, or choir singer in your parish. If you want to become better versed in the Catholic faith, attend RCIA classes. Consider becoming an active member of the church's chapter of the Knights of Columbus or Legion of Mary. These organizations include faith-filled men and women who become dear friends. They pray the rosary at meetings and help those in need.

You might consider reading Pastor Max Lucado's *Daily Devotionals*. Another one of his books, *Anxious for Nothing: Finding Calm in a Chaotic World,* looks at diminishing anxiety with faith and is informative. Your faith and prayer recitation can become an essential part of your life. Ideally, develop the habit of beginning and ending the day in prayer.

Rely on your faith and Catholic brothers and sisters to cope with the unexpected illnesses and tragic deaths of dear family members and friends. Mass attendance can bring tranquility, as does saying the rosary. The rosary is one of our most cherished prayers for the intercession of the Blessed Mother. Praying the rosary strengthens your faith, growing spiritually, being comforted, and helping those for whom you pray.

Say prayers to Jesus, Mother Mary, and the saints who will intercede on your behalf for improved mental health. Remember that Jesus is by your side always. Pray to Saint Raphael and Saint Dymphna who are the patron saints of those struggling with mental illness; they understand your pain and burden.

God, Treatment, and Therapy

Belief in God and active church participation lead to more significant gains in overall mental health and well-being. This is especially the case over any course of treatment for depression. Your beliefs, church activities, and therapy can lead to healing from depression and other mental illnesses.

Researchers consistently report that those who strongly believe in God and take part in faith-based activities are buffered from mental illness.

Harvard and Stanford-educated psychologist and writer Sonja Lyubomirsky, Ph.D., in her book, *The How of Happiness* (2007), states that enhancing your association with religion and spirituality improves your well-being and happiness. The practice of religion, with a focus on private prayer and collective worship, can engender hope, gratitude, love, awe, compassion, joy, and even ecstasy.

Lyubomirsky and other researchers affirm that spiritual people are happier than nonspiritual people, have superior mental health, cope better with stressors, have more satisfying marriages, use drugs and alcohol less often, are physically healthier, and live longer lives.

She further notes that people for whom spirituality is central in their lives experience a sense of the divine in their day-to-day existence. For example, they actively cultivate feelings of inspiration and wholeness by fostering a sense of God's love, which is the most significant predictor of happiness.

More action, however, is needed. How you look at life's challenges and spend your waking hours will color your points of view and actions. Examples include, for example, minimalism, the use of social media, and physical exercise.

Minimalism

Pope Francis states, "We are the bearers of gratitude and hope. Let us be thankful for what we have. We shall never have enough if we concentrate on what we do not have." Everyone can receive help from the pope's wisdom.

Minimalism is about leading a meaningful life by avoiding the unnecessary. It includes the refusal of social conformity with the compulsion to buy things. It is about simplicity, utility, and elegance. It is about "less is more," embracing the most of fewer things. The most common misconception is that minimalists suffer and sacrifice while having fewer things and less exciting experiences. This is simply untrue.

Minimalism denies social expectations, and a minimalist lifestyle involves living with fewer resources or things, whether in terms of houses or possessions. It is a part of the thought process of how a person chooses to live with the minimal things in life and yet be satisfied and happy. A minimalist lifestyle is by no means a radical lifestyle but rather an optimal one.

Consider reading *Minimalism: Live a Meaningful Life* (2016) by Joshua Fields Millburn and Ryan Nicodemus for guidance. In your reading, you may agree with and wish to live by their ideas about health practices, healthy relationship pursuit, passions in life, personal growth, and using your life to contribute to others.

The Millburn & Nicodemus book is an informative read and may remind you of what is truly important for you: to live a wholesome and meaningful life. It is available on Amazon.com. The authors also have minimalism-content videos on YouTube. You may wish to embrace the adage that things important to you are not necessarily things.

In closing, minimalism does not suggest that you live a life without comforts and beautiful things. If you have been successful in your life pursuits, please enjoy the benefits of your labors with a beautiful home, late model vehicles, international travel, and the absolute best for your children. You have earned them.

Minimalism, however, advocates living within your means, budgeting your income, and eliminating or reducing your credit card or other debt. At a minimum, have at least a month's savings in the bank for emergencies and learn to enjoy the simple things in life. Doing so allows you to be generous to yourself, children, the church, extended family members, and close friends.

Social Media

Social network sites are ubiquitous and constitute a standard tool for interacting with others in daily life. While popular with over two hundred fifty million daily users in the United States in 2023, consider limiting your participation in social media. You do not need Facebook, Instagram, Twitter, TikTok, or Snapchat accounts. Become one of only a handful of people you know who does not spend time on social media. These hours are poorly spent time and rarely help your emotional growth.

Aside from the entertaining and invasive Chinese-owned TikTok that collects personal data with your every keystroke, Facebook is supposed to lead to new and improved relationships, information sharing, and social support. However, it leads to unrealistic comparisons that cause envy and addiction and depresses some users.

Research in 2023 shows that people spend over an hour each day just on Facebook, with frequent brief visits during the day and the evening. Over ninety-eight percent of Facebook users in the United States access the website using their mobile devices. Could this interrupting, distracting, and sometimes anxiety-producing activity be spent in better ways?

Perhaps you could give up your daily hour on Facebook for Lent. We know that the main purpose of "giving up" things for Lent is to bring us closer to God; to prioritize God; to put God in the center of our minds and lives; to make God the focal point.

Researchers report that daily Facebook use leads to declines in subjective well-being in young adults, especially those between eighteen and thirty-four. It seems odd that Facebook was supposed to be a platform for social connections and friendship building.

Aside from these declines, the Federal Bureau of Investigation (FBI) reports in 2023 that one-half million predators are on the internet with false Facebook profiles or use Instant messaging and chat rooms to pose as threats to children daily.

Only fifteen percent of parents know what their pre-teen and teenage children are doing on Facebook.

Predators' common goals are to receive sexual images from children and eventually meet them. Facebook, instant messaging, and chatrooms are where over eighty percent of child sex crimes begin.

Researchers in 2022 reported that one in every twenty-five children was manipulated into physical contact within a year of grooming. These children, usually aged twelve to fifteen, are most often targeted by online predators. The pandemic has led to over twenty-one million confirmed enticements or "catfishing" cases by mostly men pursuing girls and young adolescent women.

Many parents are not adequately communicating with, or protecting, their children from this evil. Setting rules for children and their social media activities and creating a positive environment that allows children to share if a problem arises are essential to keeping them safe from online predators.

The wiser users on Facebook only use the platform to share information, photos, and life experiences with a small, closed, and private group of family members and friends. Pictures and kind messages are shared with a few family members and friends. If your Facebook page is an amiable private platform for a limited number of special family members and friends, continue its use. But be vigilant.

Is Facebook bothering you? Carefully monitor and consider reducing your time on it and other social media.

Monitor your feelings during and after social media use. After an hour on Facebook, do you feel better or worse? Is your mood improved? If Facebook use brings you laughter and a closeness with others, continue its use. But perhaps you can supplement your use with telephone calls, email messages, or visits to the family member or good friend to connect further.

Visit the internet for research on the national mental health decline and the risks associated with Facebook use. The research is found on Google Scholar and published in high-impact journals by academic researchers and scholars at our Ivy League universities studying Facebook addiction, Facebook depression, and Facebook envy. Researchers report a decline in educational and work performance resulting from its extensive use.

Mental health experts suggest that your time on social media platforms should be limited to ten minutes daily. Researchers consistently report that those who do not engage in social media have better mental health than those who spend hours on the platforms. For those of you who are depressed, consider limiting your Facebook and other social media use.

Recognize that social media platforms like your Facebook, TikTok, Twitter, Snapchat, and Instagram accounts are often distorted versions of reality.

These media platforms are also invasive data collectors of your more personal information and buying preferences. They conduct website content tracking by digitally accessing your cell phones, laptops, and other digital devices.

Through your actions, your personal and family privacy is becoming obsolete. Social boundaries are becoming reduced leading to data sale and misuse, online security breaches, and personal financial vulnerability. You are wise to monitor and reduce your use.

Facebook and all social media platforms could be more responsible and promote all users' mental health information via mental health education. Messages could include warnings about the platforms' abuse, misuse, overuse, and addiction.

The National Suicide Prevention Hotline (NSPH) at 800-273-8255, 988, or text "Hello" to 741741 is one of a dozen hotlines. NSPH received 2,390,000 or over sixty-five hundred calls each day in 2020. The numbers are increasing by ten percent each year. The calls are anonymous and save lives.

There are other telephone numbers for crisis counseling. These numbers can be reached 24/7/365:

- 988 Suicide and Crisis Lifeline, 988, 800-273-8255

- Trevor Lifeline for LGBT Youth, 866-488-7386

- Trans Lifeline, 877-565-8860

- RAINN National Sexual Assault Hotline, 800-656-4673

Trained personnel on these hotlines are available 24/7/365 and ready to listen. These helping professionals can also guide you to mental health services in your community. Do not hesitate to text or call. Hotlines save lives and direct callers to local mental health services.

Too often, people are hesitant to call law enforcement which can supply emergency services 24/7/365. A call to 911 can be a lifesaver for those who are a danger to themselves or others, appear to be overdosing, or require an ambulance resulting from a self-inflicted injury or experiencing a mental health crisis. Law enforcement has crisis intervention training for its officers, and often social workers are on paid staff who can help.

The preoccupation with death and suicide, sometimes referred to as "suicide ideation," can sometimes be a problem among those who are depressed. The topic, research, and its multiple suicide scales and measurements are published in the National Library of Medicine (NLM) and PubMed Central. Even worse, depressed people often make suicide attempts.

A person dies by suicide every eleven minutes in the United States.

According to the CDC, forty-six thousand were killed by their own hands in 2020, and the number increases yearly. For a more comprehensive view of mental illness statistics, including suicide, visit the CDC website and look for the "Fast Facts" on mental health. The statistics are alarming.

A portion of those who succumb to suicide are Catholics. The *Catechism of the Catholic Church* states in paragraph 2283 that, "We should not despair of the eternal salvation of persons who have taken their own lives. By ways known to Him alone, God provides the opportunity for salutary repentance. The Church prays for persons who have taken their own lives." These are comforting words to those of us who have lost family members to suicide.

Fortunately, by the joint efforts of Bishop and Ministry Chaplain John P. Dolan in the Diocese in Phoenix and Deacon Ed Shoener in Scranton's Diocese, the "Association of Catholic Mental Health Ministries" was recently established. The ministry is a response to parish members and their families struggling with mental illness and suicide.

The ministry provides compassionate films, books, and newsletters found with an internet browser search. The ministry supports parishes and dioceses in educating interested church members about mental health and mental illness to provide spiritual support for those with mental illness and those who care for them.

Guns, the Constitution's Second Amendment, and gun control are in the news daily and though they tend to get less public attention than gun-related homicides, "suicide by gun" has long accounted for most suicide deaths in the United States.

In 2020, fifty-four percent of all gun-related deaths in the nation were suicides at over twenty-four thousand, while forty-three percent were murders at nineteen thousand, according to the CDC. The remaining gun deaths in 2020 were categorized as "unintentional," "involving law enforcement," or "undetermined circumstances."

Suicide by a firearm is a commonplace method for suicide in the United States.

If you are depressed and suffer from chronic thoughts of suicide, please have your guns removed from your home and do not purchase a firearm.

Even with the gun control chatter in the news, on the opinion pages, and with Congress members of the frequent school and neighborhood shootings, gun use for killing is a growing problem in America. There are no simple solutions to our deaths-by-guns in our uncivil and divided society.

The Journal of the American Medical Association (JAMA) published a distressing gun-related research article in 2021. The persons who drove the gun buying surge in 2020 were those who bought a firearm for the first time.

It is alarming that these first-time weapons buyers in 2020 also reported past month's suicide thoughts, a precursor to suicide attempts. The large research sample population of adults lived in New Jersey, Minnesota, and Mississippi.

There is a need for hotlines as suicide was the second leading cause of death in 2019 for people ages ten to thirty-four and the fourth leading cause of death for people ages thirty-five to forty-four. Suicide is most profound for our vulnerable young, the LGBTQ+ community, Black teens, and Native Americans. Some of this mental health distress comes from comparisons on social media and FOMO or "fear of missing out."

Physical Exercise

Whatever your age, there is strong scientific evidence that being physically active can help you lead a healthier and happier life. People who exercise regularly have a lower risk of developing long-term conditions, such as heart disease, Type 2 Diabetes, and some cancers.

Exercise is a miraculous low-cost or free medicine for those suffering from depression, and mental health providers should more widely prescribe it to clients and patients. Dozens of scientific population-based studies, clinical studies, and meta-analytic reviews on exercise and mental health confirm that exercise reduces depression.

Therapists should encourage exercise activities with depressed patients regardless of their Body Mass Index. Rather than prescribing the popular antidepressants like Zoloft or Wellbutrin, psychiatrists should prescribe appropriate exercise routines or combine the psychotropic with a prescription for daily exercise.

Exercise improves your mood. Try it for a week or two. It can include activities at a wellness center, gardening, mowing the lawn, or working around the house or apartment by vacuuming or sweeping.

You may enjoy walking on a treadmill or stepping on the Stairmaster in a gym setting. Enjoy brisk walks on the indoor track and laps in the indoor or outdoor pool. Exercise with free weights.

Exercise three or four mornings each week with a family member or colleague. You will always feel healthier and more alive after workouts.

Obesity

"Obese" and "obesity" are unpopular words rarely uttered in our daily conversation, even in clinical medical settings. They are shaming words in the American lexicon. Euphemisms like chubby, plump, heavy, and oversized are kinder and gentler descriptors for excess weight.

In our post-pandemic world, obesity rates are climbing fast. *Metabolism*, a prestigious global medical journal, reported in 2022 that China, Japan, South Korea, and India had the lowest rates of obesity, while the United States, Russia, Mexico, and Turkey had the highest rates of obesity. The United States continues to be the most obese nation in the world.

Obesity is a severe medical problem in the United States and is strongly associated with depression. According to the National Institutes of Health (NIH), obesity is a chronic disease that affects four in ten adults, and one in ten Americans has severe obesity.

Morbidly obese people have a BMI of over forty. They often find difficulty climbing flights of stairs, walking distances, and doing chores around the house like vacuuming, floor mopping, or window cleaning.

Being obese leads to osteoarthritis, diabetes, heart disease, gout, stroke, lower back pain, hip and knee joint pain, and fungal rashes in the fatty skin folds. The excess weight adversely influences the knees, hips, and lower back. Obesity sometimes leads to painful surgery for pain and joint problems.

According to research published in PubMed Central's *International Orthopaedics,* obesity increases the likelihood of total joint replacement surgery, even among younger adults. A portion of the knee and hip replacements could be prevented with a BMI of less than thirty-one, and often joint pain is reduced or vanishes with weight loss.

According to reliable research, depression is the most significant medical problem associated with a larger BMI.

We quickly agree that heart disease, diabetes, and alcoholism are diseases. We must also recognize that obesity is a disease, and its prejudice must be named and removed. Obesity causes depression and other mental illnesses and should be treated without discrimination and in a caring and compassionate manner. There is no room for judgment. Look through the lens of understanding as you see an obese person.

A variety of practical and societal factors can lead to depression for those living with obesity. These include:

Quality of life. Those who carry extra weight often face problems related to physical and occupational functioning. This is due to a larger size and chronic ailments. Being physically unable to do the things they love, including attending fun and physically active events, traveling, or visiting with friends and family, leads to social isolation, loneliness, and increased difficulty coping with life's hardships.

Weight discrimination. There has been a trend in TV reality talk shows for morbidly obese women in spandex tights to celebrate their sizes while minimizing the medical risks. A positive self-image is critical to mental health. However, overweight people are wise to deal with the opposing views on obesity.

Weight discrimination refers to the stereotypical attitudes that define people and some see obese people as lacking personal discipline in their food consumption. Negative misperceptions are often widespread among peers in the workplace and clinical settings among healthcare providers. These attitudes lead to discriminatory behaviors that affect a person's self-esteem, employment opportunities, and healthcare quality.

Physiological issues. There are obesity-related health factors that can negatively influence mental health. Research suggests that excess body fat and poor eating habits increase body inflammation. Heightened inflammation leads to a higher risk of developing depression and plays a role in adversely affecting the immune system's health.

While excess weight can adversely affect a person's emotional well-being, mental health conditions may influence their weight. Examples include:

- Chronic stress, anxiety, depression, and mental health conditions like bipolar disorder may cause someone to use food to cope. They also make poor dietary choices which, in turn, cause weight gain.
- A serotonin deficiency linked with depression and anxiety is reported to lead to cravings for simple carbohydrates. Simple carbohydrates include candy, sugared sodas, donuts, and cakes. People who lack serotonin often self-medicate with food.
- Those who are depressed sometimes lack the energy or desire to exercise or participate in other physical activities. An inactive lifestyle leads to weight gain, and

behavioral change is difficult. But becoming more active can lead to weight loss, improved physical health, and feeling better.

Treatments for obesity can pose obstacles. For example, pharmacotherapies can be used to treat the symptoms of depression. But the drawback is that select antidepressants and mood stabilizers can cause **weight gain.** This is widely known. People already struggling with excess weight avoid seeking prescription treatment for depression for fear they will gain even more weight.

Mental illness poses an added barrier to living a healthier lifestyle for overweight people. Traditional weight-management therapies, such as following a nutritional plan or a physical activity regimen, may be difficult for someone already struggling with depression. Depressed people usually do not want to exercise or focus on dietary strategies. Often when they do, the actions are temporary, which is why a support system and medical guidance are essential.

Act now, as there are readily available treatment solutions for obesity.

Evidence-based obesity health care includes positive psychology therapy, guidance by a registered dietician (RD), prescription anti-obesity medications, and, in limited cases, bariatric surgery.

Anti-obesity medicines can also help reduce the risk of heart disease, diabetes, osteoarthritis, and other complications. Obesity and depression can be treated simultaneously through effective therapy and medical treatment by caring medical providers and therapists.

Regular moderate aerobic exercise can help to reduce weight and BMIs. Walking around with less excess weight feels good. Losing weight improves a person's appearance and boosts their self-image and mood. Even dropping ten percent of body weight makes a person feel and look better.

Through the years, you learn that weight loss and weight constancy are not a sprint of weeks but a marathon that takes months and even years of thoughtful, careful eating and exercise. It includes checking your daily activity and food intake and choosing healthy foods and drinks.

Millions in the United States suffer from food addiction and compulsive overeating. These behaviors often result directly from low self-esteem, making the person vulnerable to negative peer pressure, multiple addictions, and binge eating.

Those who have a problem with food consumption can receive help from membership in Overeaters Anonymous (OA), a 12-step program without cost. OA is a global community of millions who support each other in recovering from compulsive eating behaviors. They welcome anyone who feels they have a problem with food.

OA is a life-changing program with hundreds of daily meetings online and in person in most towns and cities across the United States. Their literature is helpful, and OA can be reached by visiting their Overeaters Anonymous website or calling them in New Mexico at 505-891-4320. It is encouraging to hear from OA members who have lost hundreds of pounds and have kept the weight off for years. It works for those who work the program.

Relationships

Relationships are fundamental to your health and well-being and influence your mental health and the risk of depression. Supportive, warm, and caring relationships lead to a longer and healthier life. A recent Gallup poll found that people who reported they have friends and family to rely on were more satisfied with their health than people who felt isolated.

Try to rebuild the emotionally distant relationships with your spouse, partner, or children. Please stop if you are dismissing or hurting them with what you say and do. It is not your job, the pursuit of title and money, or handsome things; your spouse and children should come first in your life. If they do not, do something. Make them your priority; be available for them. Listen to them. Reserve your criticism. And be compassionate.

If you are verbally or physically abusive to your loved ones, go to confession, and discuss these transgressions with your priest. Seek his advice and absolution. You will also benefit by entering weekly or biweekly individual and family counseling. Damaged relationships separate us from God, but reparation is possible.

Use the lens of love with your dear ones. Read the *Bible* verses that speak to you about family love. Pray for reconciliation in damaged family relationships and improved healthy relationships.

Forgiveness is a personal character strength. Forgive those who have hurt you. As you recite the Lord's prayer at Mass, with the rosary, and in your private conversations with Jesus, reflect on the words of "how we have trespassed (sinned) against others, and how they have trespassed (sinned) against us."

Forgive the person for their unkind or hurtful acts or words. Your forgiveness relieves the painful mental chatter ruminating over past hurts and your resentments toward others. Pray for those who have hurt you.

All of us have made both serious and minor mistakes in our relationships with others. And these mistakes cause us shame and guilt. But you can seek forgiveness through honest and contrite conversations with these people. Meet with them, apologize, and ask for their forgiveness. If you are unable to meet with them, pray for them.

In your pursuit of forgiveness, light a church votive candle and have a Mass said for them.

Learn to forgive yourself for your transgressions. You are imperfect. Pray that you do not repeat your mistakes. Each time you forgive yourself and others, it becomes easier to do so the next time. You are gradually changing your habit of forgiveness in a way that brings you peace of mind.

We are often our worst critics. One of the greatest gifts you can give yourself is to forgive yourself for your mistakes. Learning to forgive yourself leads to improved mental health.

It may initially feel uncomfortable but learn to pray with your family members. These prayers can be simple expressions of thanksgiving at each meal. Say prayers of thanks when a family member receives a promotion, a merit bonus, gets a decent school report card, or is successful in a sports event.

If you are a parent with pre-teen and adolescent children, focus on communication. Recognize that being a young person in the 2020 decade is complicated. Young people now have non-stop media exposure filled with "situational" morals where naming right from wrong is often clouded. This clouding confuses them. Guide them kindly in making the right decisions.

Hormonal changes and puberty can be even more stressful for youth today when appearance seems crucial.

Also, parents may sometimes place unhealthy elevated academic and athletic expectations on their children. These heightened expectations can cause a strain on younger people.

Bullying, depression, self-harm, and suicide attempts have become more common among elementary, middle, and high school students in the 2020 decade. The school nurses, counselors, school psychologists, and behavioral specialists make a valiant effort to meet the students' mental health needs, but they are grossly understaffed.

Classroom teachers in the nation's public school divisions are pleading with their school superintendents and school boards for more aid with behavioral and educational problems in these post-pandemic times.

Those adults who are in our classrooms or visit the classrooms will observe that one or two students in each classroom today are resistant to cooperatively listening to their teachers, taking part in the classroom teaching-learning process, and doing assigned homework. These students disrupt teaching and learning in the classrooms for all the students.

More instructional assistants are needed in the classrooms, lunchrooms, and school playgrounds for improved discipline. These assistants should be paid a livable wage and certainly more than local fast-food restaurant servers.

The declining national educational test scores in high school science, mathematics, and English reading are a sad testament to education in the United States. South Korea, Slovenia, Japan, Poland, Canada, and China are a few of the twenty-four countries that surpass our students in test performance.

The scores are a product of the nation's indefensible shorter-length school years and the more limited student and parent commitment to learning in the elementary, middle, and high schools. It is not due to the teachers' commitment or efforts in the classroom or public education costs.

Just as the parents are the first educators for a child's prayer life, their Catholic education, and participation in the sacraments, they have a responsibility for their children's school education. This parental responsibility includes school and classroom behavior expectations, the children's completion of homework, and ongoing communication with, and support of, the classroom teachers and school administration.

American society must make a more significant investment in the education of our youth. Added educators, a more extended school year, and enhanced mental health continuing education for school administration, classroom teachers, and staff members are needed in our schools.

If your child seems depressed, contact your child's pediatrician, teacher, and school nurse, and pursue a therapist in the community for individual and family therapy.

We want our youth to succeed in high school, enter colleges, trade schools, the military, or some form of voluntary service, and learn a profession or trade. They are the future leaders and we want our youth to become gainfully employed in meaningful endeavors.

Tragically, as of 2022, more men and women reside in America's jails and prisons than wear military uniforms on active duty in our U.S. armed forces.

A caring education system that discourages dropping out and includes excellent mental health counseling could curb the number of dropouts and offenders and interrupt the post-high school "pipeline to prison" by young adults.

The "school-to-prison pipeline" is a term often used to describe the connection between exclusionary school punishments like suspensions and expulsions and eventual involvement in the criminal justice system. Black and Hispanic students are far more likely than white students to be suspended or expelled, and Black and Hispanic Americans are disproportionately represented in the nation's prisons. The research is irrefutable.

Researchers report that completing more school years reduces the likelihood of later criminal activity. Enrollment in uncrowded and schools that have proper academic and humanistic resources leads to graduation from high school. These all lead to reduced later criminal activity.

There are things you can do now. If you have children in school, encourage them to complete their education. Discuss school activities and assignments with them. And encourage them to read for homework and pleasure.

Please get to know their teachers personally and introduce yourself to the school principal and assistant principals. Communicate with their teachers via email messaging, calling them, and written notes. Become an interested, supportive, and involved parent.

Arrange to visit their school and observe in the classrooms as a visiting guest and teacher's aide for a few days. The scheduled school "parent-teacher days" are too often empty school days with teachers waiting for parents to visit. Be the rare parent who attends all the school parent-teacher conferences and parent assemblies.

Become more active in your children's education because your children are worth the investment in time and energy. Visiting and engaging in school activities is often an awakening experience for most parents.

An effective, cooperative, and supportive parent-teacher relationship is a gift to your children in school.

Regardless of parental status and your children's schooling, it is critical that you choose your friends wisely. Just as you carefully check your children's circle of friends, associate with those people who boost your mood and have positive attitudes about life. Choose those who smile often and are enthusiastic and optimistic. Avoid those who see the darkness rather than the light.

Associate with those who would agree with the decades-old slogan that "the glass is half full rather than half empty." This is attributed to JFK's U.S. Peace Corps establishment and promotion in the early 1960s, a government-funded agency that is still globally-reaching and, in 2023, reinvigorated and vibrant today in over one hundred countries.

"The good life" is filled with smiles and laughter and a realization that each of us is blessed with grace, which is God's unconditional love for us. Through grace, God works to change our hearts and lives. We are guided in our relationships through the Holy Spirit's counsel and guidance.

Do not boast about your Catholic faith, as your actions and how you treat others reveal your faith in action.

And in your actions, do not pursue recognition from others for your charitable deeds. Quietly give your financial and other gifts anonymously. Anonymous gifts are the finest gifts.

It matters how you treat others, including your community's homeless, hungry, jailed, and disenfranchised. Can you name specific ways you have helped- and continue to help- those in need through your volunteer activities and money?

Consider the people in your life and think about how they affirm you. They are accepting of themselves and you. They are kind and hesitate to judge or criticize. Think about actions you can take to enhance your relationships. Schedule a time to connect with a few friends daily by visits or via Zoom, telephone, text messaging, or email. The church is a beautiful place to connect with others at Mass.

To enhance your well-being, you need people who emanate a cheerful outlook through their kindness and emotional support. We all need people who strengthen our mental health and contribute to our lives. They may not number many, but they are essential.

Be thoughtful about those with whom you spend your time. Surround yourself with a few friends and acquaintances who enhance your mood. If you do not have any good friends, look for them through involvement in your church, a civic organization like the Rotary, or a volunteer association like Habitat for Humanity.

Newscasts

The news content is often depressing and can bring anxiety even to the most buoyant and happy person. Aside from the economic woes, we hear about the frequent school shootings by crazed persons with easily purchased assault rifles. Even elementary school children are wielding weapons and wounding teachers in 2023.

We may worry about the wildfires in California, increased regional droughts affecting farm crop yields, flooding throughout the country, and other natural disasters. These and more are brought on by global warming.

You may feel obligated to scan the daily newspaper or watch national and global news snippets on your television or laptop as an informed member of society. However, you need not know the details of everything happening in the nation and the world.

It is wise to limit your news watching to about sixty minutes daily.

Listen to the news on the non-profit National Public Radio (NPR) and scan your local town newspaper. Refrain from wasting time listening to the cable news with self-important talking heads with little insight or expertise. News story repetition and silly TV and radio commercials are annoying to experience.

Sadly, news reporting as a discipline has evolved to include infused opinions by talking heads. What would the news journalists of decades ago say about today's news reporting?

In 2023, the popular term "truth decay" joined our U.S. English lexicon, which includes phrases like "fake news" and "alternative facts." Fake news has also joined "fake science" manufactured by climate change deniers and anti-vaxxers. We have "fake history" promoted by the antisemite Holocaust revisionists and white supremacists.

Many would suggest that truth has died with the never-ending misleading news stories. It has become acceptable and unsurprising for state and national leaders to exaggerate and lie in public forums. If repeated often enough, like the fictitious presidential election results, outright lies eventually become "truths" to the gullible and easily-persuaded few.

Polarized and hate-infused reporting has become standard. With smiles, the newscasters repeatedly present the sad and horrific events occurring in our lives and those around the globe. Also, much of what you hear and read is not newsworthy. It is filler for the bored.

We cannot control other people's lives that we hear and read about in the news. So how does the information help us? It hardly enlightens us, and it is fodder for complaining. Nor do we control the political chaos in Ukraine, Syria, the South China Sea, or the Persian Gulf.

Sophisticated communication technologies continue to evolve, and the news is now immediate. We learn instantly what is happening in even the more remote sectors of the world.

For those who insist on watching or listening to news programs for hours, it is suggested that you actively seek local stories where you could make a personal contribution to your community. There are volunteer opportunities for you mentioned in the local newscasts. There are volunteer opportunities in all communities across the nation. Seek a non-profit agency that helps the refugees, the homeless, or the hungry.

Perhaps you are baffled by those who sit in front of the television, binge-watch Fox or CNN news, and shout at the screens. These habits are well-paved avenues to depression. It is fodder for complaints, judgments, and unhappiness. The news about politics, politicians, and political strife often focuses on things over which we have little control.

If you sit for hours in front of a TV and surf Fox, CNN, MSNBC, or CBS, treat these channels like the offerings on a food buffet table. If you choose to dine, be selective in your choices. Do you care to eat the mushy brussels sprouts, overcooked dry chicken, or stale white bread slices descriptive of most news agency offerings today?

You may wonder about the opinion writers in the local and national forum pieces in print newspapers. Some opinion writers take delight from their home armchairs in exacting character assassination on our leaders and their families. How unhappy and angry these pundits must be to believe that their biting criticism somehow showcases their own intellect, knowledge, or education. It does not.

Who cares to drink their sour milk writings? Could these critics be moved by God's grace to write about the constructive contributions of our leadership? Or perhaps, with compassion, could they suggest ways to strengthen our communities and the nation by better caring for the tens of millions of the disenfranchised in our society? If Jesus were to join them as a co-author, what would these critics write?

These wordsmiths would benefit from the application of the PERMA Model elements and Golden Rule Adherence in their lives which are discussed in later chapters. Be selective in what and who you read.

Do you know anyone who constantly complains? Do you enjoy listening to them complain about "anything" like taxes, their health problems, or government agencies or "anyone" like our legislators, educators, law enforcement officers, or health service providers? These chronic complainers look at life through a lens of gray shadows and unhappiness.

Their negative energy could be used in more productive ways like exercising, volunteering, visiting a library, reading an uplifting biography, or attending a faith-based service. Be kind to the complainers but avoid them whenever possible. Say prayers for them.

Physical Health

Recognize the connection between physical and mental health. See your family physician or physician extender every six months and whenever you are sick. It is wise to check your blood pressure, blood chemistries, and urine. In addition, weigh yourself weekly and watch your weight.

Good physical health is essential to healing your depression and improving your overall well-being.

Those who suffer from depression often disregard their overall health. They may rarely exercise. They overeat and often binge on sugared sodas, ice cream, potato chips, and sugary pastries. These overpriced sugary and salty goodies damage their mental and physical health. Their excessive consumption is harmful to their health.

Their unhealthy drinking of supersized quarts of highly caloric sugared sodas alone may lead to a BMI of 31— obesity. Along with being obese, they may develop stage two hypertension with 140/90+ readings and Type 2 Diabetes with 6.5+ level A1C readings. However, through their efforts and the care of effective physicians or physician extenders they trust, they can bring their weight down and bring those chronic conditions under control.

Be mindful of your diet and all your foods and drinks. Drink water during the day. Only rarely enjoy a sugared soda and abstain from diet sodas. Consume candy on special occasions as you check your A1C for diabetes and your eGFR for kidney disease stage status. Do frequent blood pressure checks and needle sticks at home for blood pressure and sugar levels.

Buy vegetables at the local food cooperative and the town farmer's market. Limit processed foods and snacks like salty pretzels and potato chips. Drink three or four pints of plain or unflavored carbonated water daily to stay hydrated. Drink even more water if you are easily overheated during the summer months. Drink more water and hydrate if you are on antidepression medicines.

Consider developing food routines with planned food purchases, diet preparation, cooking, and eating. Change is within your reach. Change starts with minor dietary changes- sugared sodas to water, pancakes with syrup to scrambled egg whites- and move to more significant nutritional changes.

Alcohol and Drugs

Alcohol consumption is very much a part of our American culture. The National Institute on Alcohol Abuse and Alcoholism

(NIAAA) states that in 2023, eighty-six percent of Americans over twenty-one drink. Of that percentage, twenty-five percent are binge drinkers. While the legal drinking age is twenty-one, binge drinking is now "normal" among seventeen-, eighteen-, nineteen-, and twenty-year-olds.

There is now a new vocabulary for excessive drinking. "High-intensity drinking" is defined as consuming alcohol at two or more times the gender-specific binge drinking thresholds of four drinks in one sitting. Visit Google Scholar to review the multiple research-based articles on high-intensity drinkers as a uniquely high-risk group.

Compared with those who choose to binge drink, these high-intensity drinkers are seventy times more likely to have an alcohol-related emergency department (ED) visit. These ED visits sometimes become medical emergencies with alcohol poisonings that require hospitalization. When alcohol is combined with prescription or recreational drugs, death can occur.

An occasional single glass of wine or a beer will be pleasant for most. It can relax and bring pleasure to those who have no predisposition to alcoholism. Drinking beer, wine, and distilled spirits serve a social function in society, and you are blessed to sit and enjoy a single drink without being compelled to drink a second, third, fourth, or fifth.

If you are struggling with depression and drinking alcoholic beverages, please pause and consider it further.

You can lead a better life without alcohol consumption. Some of us have seen alcoholism's emotional, physical, and financial damage to the family. The toll of the disease on family members cannot be measured in day-to-day stress, worry, relationship damage, disappointment, and financial costs. The wounds to the family members brought on by alcoholism can be traumatic and last a lifetime.

Alcoholism is a family disease, and an essential seminal book that can help you manage the alcoholism of, for example, an abusive parent or sibling is *Adult Children of Alcoholics* by Janet Woititz. The Woititz book, a classic, is worthy of a close read for those who live or have lived with an alcoholic. It is available in local bookstores and on Amazon.com.

If you are struggling with depression and your life is further disrupted by an alcoholic spouse, sibling, or child, you may wish to consider membership in Al-Anon as a supplement to your psychotherapy. This mutual-support organization has one purpose: to help family members of alcoholics and drug addicts deal with the problems brought on by the addictions.

Small local groups do this by practicing the Twelve Steps inside and outside of the rooms, usually in faith-based communities. Members welcome and comfort the suffering family members of alcoholics and addicts and provide understanding and encouragement to the family members in the meeting.

Al-Anon's participation is uncomplicated and informal. It has electronic, telephone, and in-person meetings throughout the day and evening. Also, Alateen can help young people who suffer from an alcoholic parent or friend. Al-Anon and Alateen can be reached on the internet with a simple browser search.

Aside from alcohol purchases, finances can be a concern. Over sixty percent of American families now report living paycheck to paycheck with little cash reserves for medical, dental, or auto repair emergencies.

It is baffling how Americans spend so much on signature beers, expensive wines, and name-brand bourbons. What portion of their take-home pay or fixed income goes to buying alcoholic beverages rather than food for the family?

What percentage of customers who visit the local supermarkets, the corner 7-11s, or ABC liquor stores are alcoholics, problem drinkers, or just social drinkers? How many are high-intensity drinkers?

Customers who fill store baskets and purchase beers, wines, and liquors might consider how much they spend each week on alcohol. Is it twenty dollars or one hundred dollars each week? Regardless of disposable income, could these dollars be spent in better ways, especially in economically challenging times?

Does their liquor drinking bring them pleasure, temporary relief, or pain regardless of the expense? Do they have misgivings after drinking alcoholic beverages?

There are solutions to the complex problem of drinking excessively. Alcoholics Anonymous, SMART, the Sinclair Method, and Cognitive Behavioral Therapy (CBT) are reliable solutions. Help can be just a telephone call or internet browser search away. They can pick up the phone or tap on the computer keyboard to get help.

Through prayer, they can ask God for help in reducing or ending their alcohol use. They can pray for His guidance. If their drinking has caused emotional or physical harm to others, they can discuss these harms in the confessional. They can join a mutual support group or attend individual and group therapy sessions at the local community mental health center like a Community Services Board.

With depression, another drug of concern is cannabis. There is a strong positive correlation between indiscriminate marijuana use and depression.

Legal cannabis use is now a craze. Most states have decriminalized and legalized marijuana, allowing adults to possess and use the substance.

On a large Native American reservation on eastern Long Island headed to the Hamptons, you can walk into one of several cannabis dispensaries and buy recreational and medicinal cannabis products if you are twenty-one or older. The products include pre-rolled joints, vapes, buds, cookies, gummies, candies, and CBD drops. The marketing and packaging of the products are creative and colorful.

Visiting a cannabis dispensary in person or online might remind a buyer of visiting a swanky chocolatier shop and selecting their favorite sweets. Like the chocolates, cannabis products seem expensive. For the 420 friends, the Washington, DC dispensaries deliver the products to the customers' residences.

Regardless of its availability, life is good without mind-altering substances like marijuana. It is, however, assuring that legal marijuana products, with their regulations and strict production quality controls, end the tragic news reports of those who overdose on fentanyl and opium-augmented cannabis sold on the streets.

Sleep

Sleep is critical to our mental health. Hopefully, you are blessed to have a restful sleep most nights. Follow a sleep hygiene routine for getting to sleep and awakening by going to bed at the same time each night. Limit your computer screen time before bed; ideally, go to bed on an empty stomach and without consuming caffeine products near bedtime.

You might begin and end your day with music by Catholic musicians like layperson John Michael Talbot and Jesuit Fr. Bob Dufford, SJ. Listen to Catholic prayers upon awakening and when going to sleep. YouTube has an assortment of hymns sung during Mass that are calming to listen to. These are habits that may bring you comfort.

"Amen" is a beautiful free app for your cell phone and laptop provided by the Augustine Institute. It supplies uplifting play content for sleep, healing, spiritual growth, and comfort. Today's prayers, evening psalms, novenas, Bible verses, and living the faith are included. Listening to "Amen" is a peaceful and comforting way to go to sleep.

Sleep deprivation and depression are intricately linked. A limited number of sleep hours, like three or four, and disturbed sleep with constant awakening, are severe health problems.

Take a moment and think about your sleep. Do you get at least six hours of sleep each night? Is it restful, and do you sleep through the night with limited pee breaks? Do you awaken refreshed or still sleepy?

If sleep is a problem, discuss it with your medical provider. Perhaps a referral to a sleep study center should be ordered for a sleep evaluation. Keep in mind that select antidepressants will disturb your sleep.

Gratitude

Awaken in the morning and be grateful. Before you put your feet on the floor, give thanks for a bed, a roof over your head, bills paid, and food on the table. Whether you live in a mansion or rent a small room in a boarding house, drive a high-end Mercedes, or take the bus, look through the lens of gratitude. Each of us has much to be grateful for.

Proust tells us to be grateful to the people who make us happy; they are the charming gardeners who make our souls blossom.

Be grateful for the kind and loving people in your life and look for the goodness in them. Say a prayer of thanks for them. Positive psychologist Ryan Niemiec suggests using the "spot-explain-appreciate process" to strengthen good relationships and repair the difficult ones.

Let us spot the strengths in our family members and friends. We can then ponder these strengths and share our observations with them. We can appreciate how they comfort us. These people and their strengths are gifts to us from God.

We fill the days with activities. Be thankful for your ability to spend the day in activities that will help others in the home, family, work, and community. Be grateful for your local parish community. Be vocal, share, and express your gratitude for these activities. Shared with your parish priest that he is a blessing to you and the parishioners.

Post-traumatic Growth

Post-traumatic growth is a concept written about by scholars in the field of psychology, and there is a wealth of knowledge on Google Scholar and PubMed.gov on the subject. The idea that a person is emotionally damaged for life by past experiences is misleading and inaccurate. People can and do grow, even after the most debilitating trauma.

Oprah Winfrey writes eloquently about post-traumatic growth and living our lives to the fullest. Read her book, *What I Know for Sure,* which supplies advice on living life to its fullest. *What Happened to You: Conversations on Trauma, Resilience, and Healing* that Oprah co-authored with physician Bruce D. Perry is also recommended.

These books can help to bring you peace and calm after trauma. They can bring you a renewed sense of personal worth. You can see your life through positive, affirming, and hopeful lenses. You may buy these books on Oprah's website or Amazon.com.

Trauma inventories have been created, researched, and published in scholarly journals. Many are found on the internet. The checklists provide us with discernment in learning how successfully we have been coping with the aftermath of trauma. Importantly, they guide us in reconstructing and strengthening our perceptions of ourselves and others.

Learn more about the Trauma Symptom Inventory at the U.S. Veterans Affairs website. Regardless of veteran status, visit this user-friendly government website to learn more about trauma and PTSD.

Let us face reality. We are not frozen in time from our past emotionally painful and traumatic experiences, no matter how severe. They have certainly influenced our lives. However, they are not barriers or excuses for our inaction or a lack of emotional growth and strength development in the following decades.

Focus and contemplate on the strengths of your parents or caregivers. Their character strengths are or were many, including love, kindness, and compassion. If your parents are deceased, remember the many happy events of your youth rather than simmer in the sad and tear-filled moments. Each of us has a choice in what we think about and care to remember.

Resilience

Resilience, also known as "grit," is the ability to withstand adversity and stress-filled events in our lives. Grit is a subject worthy of discussion about relief from depression. Being resilient does not mean we do not experience stress, emotional upheaval, and suffering, as these are unavoidable. However, resilience does give us the strength to process, work through, and overcome these hardships.

Resilience is popular in self-help and psychology literature, and many self-help books remain on the best-seller lists for years. Interestingly, eighty-five percent of people classified as wealthy, based on income and tangible assets like homes and stock portfolios, read at least one self-help or educational book per month compared to fifteen percent of those classified as poor or near poor.

Angela Duckworth, Ph.D., formerly a doctoral student of Martin Seligman, Ph.D. at the University of Pennsylvania, authored a seminal best-selling book titled *Grit: The Power and Passion of Perseverance. Grit* has sold more than one million copies worldwide since its publication in 2016, and many companies and the more progressive elementary, middle, and high schools embrace the concept.

Fortune 100 companies use the grit concepts to enhance employee satisfaction and performance. Public and private k-12 schools use them to reduce behavioral problems and improve standardized test scores. *Grit* is an informative read and is recommended.

Amit Sood, Ph.D., the Global Center for Resiliency director, is another researcher and writer who studies resilience. He provides educational programs and books on this subject. One of his books is titled *Resilient Living with Dr. Sood: Building Strength for the Difficult Days.* It was published in 2019.

The books by Duckworth and Sood are enlightening. They include concrete suggestions on how you can further develop your resilience and support the growth of resilience in others. They are easily found with a simple internet browser search and are available on Amazon.com.

Those with limited resilience are easily overwhelmed and often turn to unhealthy coping mechanisms like abusing alcohol or other drugs. Some fly into physical or emotional rages and are destructive and frightening to others. The rages can be emotionally traumatic for the victims and witnesses. Rages are often fueled by excessive alcohol or illegal stimulants like methamphetamine or crack.

Resilient people tap into their strengths and support systems to overcome challenges and work through them. Resilience gives you the strength needed to overcome hardship. Through your resilience and the kindness of others, you thrive and become a productive and contributing member of society and, importantly, strength to your family and friends.

A book that can help you to learn more about resilience and its strengthening is *Resilience: A Path to Individual Healing and Collective Thriving in an Inequitable World* by Anjuli Sherin. The author skillfully discusses the circle of resilience, the practice of joyful resilience, and ways to find joy. This author gives an insightful discussion about privilege, multiple socio-political issues facing the United States today, and practices that can lead everyone to thrive.

Be grateful. Many of us have the habit of taking things for granted in our lives. However, be thankful for remembering names, toileting yourself, walking unaided or only with a cane, communicating verbally, and feeding yourself. Remind yourself of the eight hundred thousand Americans in long-term care facilities as of 2023 who cannot.

Financial Planning and Budgeting

Money may often be the focus of your thoughts and conversations. You may feel trapped if you struggle financially and can only manage to pay your minimum monthly payments on your dozen credit cards. Living from paycheck to paycheck can be a chronic worry. Financial struggles make life arduous and stressful, leading to depression and anxiety. It is time to make a few major life decisions.

Take charge of your finances and set up and follow a family budget. As your wallet empties and the multiple credit card balances rise, find out where your money is going.

Budgeting is for everyone. Without a realistic budget, even those with six-digit salaries or generous fixed incomes can spend their way into debt. A budget forces you to consider your weekly and monthly expenses and make responsible money choices. You become fully aware of your finances.

Your family budget has your fixed and variable expenses. Do you know how much you spend on housing, groceries, household expenses, transportation, insurance, medical and dental expenses, cable and cell phone, recreational expenses, and taxes?

There are free budget sheets available on the internet to gain better control over your monthly expenses.

Banks and credit unions can help you as a facet of their customer service. Most banking institutions offer budget consultation and budgeting sheets on request.

Monthly Budget

Date: _____

Monthly income (sources and amounts):

    1. _____

    2. _____

    3. _____

Church contributions: _____

Savings: _____

Housing (mortgage/rent): _____

Utilities (electricity, gas, water, garbage pickup, other):

_____

Cable and internet: _____

Cell phone costs: _____

Groceries (food, soda, etc.): _____

Alcoholic beverages: _____

Tobacco products: _____

Household expenses: _____

Credit card names, balances, and monthly payments:

    1. _____

    2. _____

    3. _____

Transportation (monthly auto loan payments/ gasoline-diesel/auto repairs/ subway/ bus/Uber):

    1. _____

2. _____

3. _____

Insurance (health, life, auto, dental, other):

1. _____

2. _____

3. _____

Medical expenses including psychotherapy (monthly insurance premiums and copays):

1. _____

2. _____

3. _____

Prescriptions and Over-the Counter (OTC) drugs (names, costs):

1. _____

2. _____

3. _____

Dental care (cleaning, fillings, crowns, implant, dentures):

_____

Recreational dining out (grande and venti coffee drinks, alcoholic drinks, recreational drugs, other):

_____

Reading Materials (Sunday newspapers, magazines, novels, other):

_____

Taxes (property and home): _____

Lottery Tickets: _____

If you are experiencing acute financial pressures in 2023 with increased health, food, medical, and housing costs, downsize with your bigger expense items like vehicles and housing if necessary. No longer use your credit cards or use them only as a convenience with the intention of paying them off as soon as possible.

Recognize the difference between a "need" and a "want" in your purchasing practices.

Do you need all those TV and cable streaming services or another pair of new dress shoes? Can you justify the purchase of the latest higher-end Android or iPhone purchased on credit with your credit card?

Before you spend money on anything else, be sure that your income covers housing, food, utilities, and transportation. Putting living expenses on credit cards is a temporary solution that creates a permanent problem.

Seek debt relief. There are non-profit agencies that can help you with downsizing your debt. You might even consider Chapter 7 bankruptcy if your medical, dental, and credit card debts are now overwhelming and a source of depression and anxiety. Discuss the matter with an attorney who specializes in bankruptcy law. While not ideal, bankruptcy is a workable solution for those seeking debt relief and a fresh start.

Finally, cut down on your spending. Learn to spend less and save more. For example, go three days without spending ten dollars each day on a large designer coffee or latte and a pastry, or a Red Bull© and a snack.

Mindfulness

Mindfulness reduces forgetfulness. Have you forgotten people's names after meeting them? Do you still rely on your GPS to visit places you have previously visited? Do you forget to take your medicines and vitamins before leaving home?

Do you constantly misplace your car keys, TV remote, and eyeglasses? Do you often worry if you have turned off the coffee pot or locked the door when you go outdoors? You may blame these incidents on a busy mind or "senior moments" and aging. This is not true.

Mindfulness puts an end to these annoyances and much more by you becoming conscious of the moment. It is a matter of focusing on what you are doing and not living in the past or the next moment but living in the "now."

There are many ways to practice mindfulness. One example is taking the time to experience and focus on your environment with all your senses- touch, sound, sight, smell, and taste. For example, when you lock the door or turn off the coffee pot, take a moment and focus on your action. You might even say, "I'm locking the door." or "I'm turning off the coffee pot." It may seem obtuse or odd, but you learn that it is effective.

Mindfulness is the conscious act of living in the moment and bringing open, accepting, and discerning attention to your actions.

It also includes looking for joy in simple life pleasures. Take a deep breath and close your eyes when you have negative thoughts. Focus on your breath as it moves in and out of your body. Slow deep breathing for even a minute can bring calmness. You can also try more structured mindfulness exercises, including mindful eating, mindful driving, and single tasking.

Listen to affirmation recordings by Bob Baker and Louise L. Hay every morning. Visit YouTube and watch videos on relaxation and stretching. In addition, do breathing exercises during quiet moments of the day. Slow deep breathing that fills your belly and chest increases your energy levels, reduces muscle tension, and reduces stress.

Many tout the benefits of multitasking. However, it is contrary to mindfulness. Multitasking may seem a terrific way to get a lot done simultaneously. But research shows that our brains are not as good at handling multiple tasks as we think.

Recent research in *Cerebrum and Human Communications Research* suggests that multitasking hampers our productivity by reducing our comprehension, attention, and overall performance of the tasks. One might wonder if those who multitask are doing quality or shoddy work.

Meditation

Meditation is a mind-body practice that can bring moments of calm. It enhances self-awareness and allows people to stay connected with themselves. When practicing meditation, the Nation Center for Complementary and Integrative Health (NCCIH) suggests focusing on the interaction between the brain, mind, body, and behavior, with your goal of moving into a peaceful and energized state of mind.

Visit the NCCIH, an NIH federal government website, and examine the "Health Topics A-Z" section for more information on mediation and other health-related matters. For example, the discussion on "headaches" is illuminating and can guide those who suffer from chronic migraines to look for the most effective treatments.

There are several types of meditation, but most share four key characteristics: a quiet location, a comfortable body position with sitting or lying down, focusing your attention, and having an open attitude.

Savor your morning and nighttime routines. Rather than your mind rambling about the past "should haves" and "could haves" over which you have no control or fretting about potential problems in the future, engage in meditation which helps you return to the present moment.

Your mind and body become quiet when you meditate. Coupled with practicing mindfulness, meditation brings peace of mind. It is the practice of profoundly focusing the mind and promoting relaxation and an enhanced sense of inner peace. It quiets your internal unending chatter. It brings calm to your body and mind for a little while. You discover the benefits of meditation if you try it.

There are diverse ways to meditate. You can sit in your favorite chair or slowly walk down a quiet street. With soft, deep breathing and a few minutes of calmness daily, meditation can slow down and even curb the mood swings that may trouble you daily.

There are many types of meditation, including, for example, Buddhist, Zen, and Vipassana. However, the most researched and proven most effective is Transcendental Meditation (TM). YouTube has TEDx Talks on TM and dozens of books on this subject on Amazon.com. Simply said, TM is the most researched meditation and most effective.

Visit the reputable "Healthline" webpage for excellent information about mediation practices for adults and children. Visit the TM website for detailed information and the cost of your area's personalized one-on-one and small group sessions.

Social Connections

Do you often feel lonely or disconnected from family members and those around you? According to a national survey published in 2022, loneliness levels have reached an all-time high across the United States.

One-half of U.S. adults report they sometimes or always "feel alone" and "socially disconnected." Nearly half also say they often think their relationships are not meaningful. The coronavirus pandemic has increased the rates of social isolation, disconnect, and loneliness.

Social isolation brings adverse health consequences. These include depression, poor sleep quality, accelerated cognitive decline, poor cardiovascular function, and impaired immunity at every stage of life. Social isolation increases your risk of premature death from every cause for every race.

Think about your methods for social enrichment and how you can reduce loneliness and isolation and better connect with others. What are they? Do you go to bars and dance clubs with friends? Do you go hiking in the mountains or visit the national parks with family members and friends? Perhaps you belong to a weekly *Bible* study group, a book or chess club, or enjoy meeting neighbors at the local farmer's market.

Your church activities can diminish your feelings of loneliness and boost your mood.

Frequent Mass attendance and rosary and prayer groups quash social isolation. Aside from the bounty of grace, these social connections prevent depression.

Value your relationships and social connections. Having close friends and family to talk with eases the pain of illness, death, and tragedies. Confiding your worries and troubles to others reduces stress and anxiety because you are no longer alone in your pain. Also, listen to and support family and friends who sound abandoned.

Rather than rush out of church after Saturday evening or Sunday Mass, take the time after the crowd leaves to introduce yourself to the parish priest and parochial vicar. Develop a personal relationship with them and talk with them outside of the confessional.

Participate in the periodic "donuts and coffee" get-togethers after Mass, the fund-raising dinners sponsored by the local Knights of Columbus chapter, and, if time allows, attend the noon weekday Masses. These are all opportunities for you to meet others and form warm, faith-based relationships.

Positive social connections protect you from loneliness. Seek out those who look through the lens of optimism. Spend time with them on fun activities. These can be as simple as sharing a meal at a restaurant after Mass, seeing an upbeat movie in the theatre with friends, or strolling in a park together.

Antidepressant and Antianxiety Medicines

Some of you may be on antidepressants and antianxiety medicines. A few of you may be contemplating a request for a prescription from your medical provider. This is a crossroads for you in your mental health care.

You may be naïve and think that medication alone can cure your depression. Sadly, you are mistaken. Besides the mild brain chemistry changes, the pills give you limited relief. They supply no tools to heal from your depression.

What the psychotropic medicines do -not- do for you include:

1. You do not learn about and develop the thinking and behavioral tools to manage your depression, stress, and anxiety.

2. The meds do not help improve your relationships with others or teach you how to build a supportive network as therapy can.

3. The meds do not improve your feelings about yourself or help you name and use your character strengths. Therapy is the place for these discussions.

4. The meds do not help you to come to terms with past traumatic experiences or, more importantly, build a hopeful, bright, and cheerful future. Again, therapy is the place for these discussions.

Your faith, church participation, care for your body, changes in your behaviors, and, importantly, effective talk therapy will help with all these issues. It is a matter of changing your thinking and behaviors and, when necessary, entering an effective therapeutic relationship with a skilled therapist.

Often, people who are depressed are prescribed antidepressants combined with antianxiety medicines. They begin and continue the medication without the benefit of therapy or making behavioral changes.

Some may even take the medications for years, but little or nothing improves in their lives. They are medicated but continue to be depressed and anxious. They learn to live as a depressed and sometimes anxious person through habit. One wonders if the medications over the years are at all helpful and perhaps simply a waste of money.

Admittedly, antidepressants and antianxiety meds are reported to supply temporary relief to many. But they should only be prescribed for limited periods and combined with frequent and regular talk therapy. Taking antidepressants without effective talk therapy and behavioral change is wasteful and ineffective.

The following chapter provides you with suggestions for your relief from depression. The chapter discusses behavioral changes and things you can do right now to improve your well-being and reduce your depression.

There is an activity at the end of each chapter of *Healing Your Depression: A Catholic Perspective, 2nd Ed.* Each activity is based on a Positive Psychology concept. Each focus on introspection, positive change, and growth through changes in viewpoints and actions. Some of these activities can be completed once; some are ideally completed weekly, monthly, or bi-annually.

The first activity is writing about a better version of yourself. Consider the elements of this better version and embrace them with an attitude of confidence. As you think about yourself, be open to the point of view of getting and feeling better.

To make progress in your well-being, you will need to imagine alternative realities- better ones- and believe that you can achieve them. This "better version" activity will be your first effort at reframing a negative to a positive mindset.

For some, the better version may lead to abrupt or gradual changes in your behaviors about your physical health. You can reduce sugar intake, consider a more balanced diet, reduce tobacco or alcohol use, see a Registered Dietitian (RD), or manage your physical health through regular exercise.

You can also consider your innermost emotional matters. Spend time thinking about the positive things you think and do, which may help you feel good about who you are. You can celebrate what is right and good about yourself and seek improvements.

It could be your strong work ethic, love towards your family members, or social and emotional intelligence. Trust that you will heal from depression and that your thoughts will become positive, hopeful, and happy.

You live a social life. A better version of yourself might include improving your relationships with your spouse or partner, children, friends, and colleagues. Might you spend more quality time with your children? You can recognize and speak proudly about the talents and accomplishments of your family members and friends.

Compliment the people around you. Learn to look through the lens of kindness and compassion rather than criticism and complaints. With reverence, you share goodness and kindness with others, and you are blessed.

God blesses you with the fruits of the Holy Spirit through your piety and acts of goodness and kindness.

Remember the *Bible* readings from Mathew, John, and Acts about the Holy Spirit and the celebrated Pentecost Sunday. You are reminded that the Holy Spirit, as recited in many of our prayers at Mass, guides and encourages you throughout the day in your decisions. The Holy Spirit helps you to shower others and yourself with love, patience, gentleness, and generosity.

With the better version, consider a variety of issues. Consider making improvements in the quality of your life at home and work. Consider how you spend money and challenge yourself with the concepts of a "need" versus a "want" regardless of disposable income. The concept of "deservedness" also arises. It is a challenge to determine a need, a want, or deserving something you are buying.

A better version challenge can include your decision to learn new skills for work or with a fun hobby.

Consider changes to your home environment. It could be something as simple as buying and tending to a potted plant for your bedroom, painting a room in your house or apartment, adding warm and bright colors to your décor, or tidying your desk drawers and closet. These simple actions can improve your mood.

You can become more active in your spiritual and religious activities. Consider how you can become more involved in your church. Can you join a weekly prayer group or serve as a reader or usher during Mass? Can you include prayer more often in your day? Are you called to volunteer with your local rescue squad, work with Habitat for Humanity, or help at the food pantry for the hungry in your community? Volunteer opportunities are many in your town or city.

Chapter Activity: Write about a better version of me.

Date: _____

Think about who I would like to become.

What qualities in myself might I strengthen for this updated version?

What qualities or activities would I like to cease doing to lead to a better me? What changes in my actions might I make in my life?

Be specific.

_____

Chapter 3

Personal Actions

*It is not the soul alone that should be healthy; if the mind is healthy
in a healthy body, all will be healthy and much better prepared to
give God greater service.*

Saint Ignatius

The Now

Today, how would you rate your mental health and your physical health? Would you describe each as excellent, good, fair, or poor? Why would you give each these rankings? Do you wish to improve both your physical and mental health?

How are you feeling now? Depressed? Anxious? Are you stressed out? Or are you content, happy, and at peace with yourself and life? Take a moment to think and feel. Close your eyes for a few moments and be in the present. Breathe deeply and slowly four or five times. Let your mind rest. You have control over your depression. Help yourself through select lifestyle changes.

Each of us is more than our history. Whether your past is filled with trauma and abuse or happiness and helping relationships, your history does not define who you are.

You are more than a job title, economic status, body size, or the number of Facebook friends or Twitter followers.

Although often inextricably linked with pride and self-value, your career and job do not define your identity. Your job title, car model, house square footage, and title do not define any of us.

Your life is your faith and spiritual practices, warm and helping relationships with people you care about, positive mental and physical health, and contributions at home, work, and community. Your life is grounded in your faith and actions.

Your life focuses on your contributions to family, friends, and community. These factors enrich you and bring you grace. While history is unchangeable, the present and future are shaped by your actions today.

Take ten minutes and create one, two, or three defined goals for yourself. Do not rush. Write about your goals and include the steps needed to succeed. Date them. The goals will have actionable steps to achieve them. Goals without actionable steps are merely dreams.

Goals with Action Steps

1. _____

2. _____

3. _____

Your lifestyle influences your mental health. Make healthy lifestyle changes to reduce your level and intensity of depression. Lifestyle practices include caring for your mind and body and involve changes in your thinking, ending harmful activities and substances that cause stress or guilt, and embracing those activities that make you feel good. It consists of taking part in healthy activities and learning new ones.

The best change is slow change. Do not attempt dramatic changes overnight or even within a week. Quick fixes do not last. Instead, start with activities you can do with little effort and work on them over the weeks, months, and years ahead.

For those interested in in-depth behavioral change research, a body of knowledge from the 1990s discusses the Transtheoretical Model and its stages of behavioral change offered by researchers Prochaska and DiClemente. Their work with drug and smoking addiction recovery is available on Google Scholar.

Behavioral Change

Your behavioral changes involve clear and thoughtful steps in your lifestyle. Behavioral changes include, for example, exercising three days each week, cessation of tobacco products, simple modifications to your diet, substance abuse elimination, and weight loss activities. Conducting stress management exercises is also a helpful behavioral change.

Ideally, you are ready to make changes in your life. You intend to start healthy behaviors now and within the following weeks. You have given thoughtful and practical consideration to the pros and cons of changing your behavior.

Pray to the Holy Spirit for His counsel and strength for you to make behavioral changes.

Examples of changes can include dietary modifications with a reduction in candy bars and salty snacks, while other changes can be a reduction in media screen time before bed. You may have reduced or ended your Facebook and other social media time. Limiting your news-watching time has improved your mood, and you may be complaining less about the news reports on local, city, state, national, and international fronts.

Behavioral change is slow and incremental. You can start by taking small steps and believing that changing your behavior will lead to a healthier life. Ideally, you have at least one significant person- a spouse, partner, or best friend- who supports you in making these changes.

Lifestyle Resolutions

If you are depressed, you are experiencing negative thinking. You may feel guilt, self-deprecation, loneliness, and anxiety. You may not want to get out of bed or leave your residence. You may have a litany of deep regrets you ruminate over with toxic "should haves" and "could haves" in your past, over which you have no control to change.

These regrets bring you down in your mood. Forgiving yourself may seem out of reach; however, long-lasting change is more likely when you refocus on positive thinking and feel hopeful about the future.

What resolutions do you have for a new life through behavioral change? Just as you prepare New Year's Resolutions, it is time to create your New Life's Resolutions. Think about and list the things you wish to change to improve your life. You control these things, including, for example, self-talk patterns, weight loss activities, and cutting recreational drug use.

New Life's Resolutions: The changes I wish to make with reasons include:

Date: _____

Changes and Reasons

1. _____

2. _____

3. _____

Specifics for Change

Focus on your comprehensive physical examination, alcohol reduction, and cannabis and recreational drug elimination to begin your self-care process. Other changes are also suggested.

Physical Examination

Your depression does not occur in a singular or isolated manner. Your health status and particular illnesses result from mental and physical fitness interplay in your body, mind, and spirit.

Your physical, mental, and spiritual health are interconnected, and care must be given to all.

Whether you have been hounded by depression for years or the mental illness began during the coronavirus pandemic, go for a complete physical exam, including blood work and urinalysis.

Physical medical problems can cause depression; ideally, you rule out any underlying maladies that can lead to symptoms of depression. For example, for a few, your depression could be brought on by something as simple as a Vitamin B deficiency or as serious as later-stage chronic kidney disease.

Your medical provider will ask about your symptoms, look for observable signs of your overall health, and ask about your medical history. The provider will also ask about your family's health history, including the history of mental illness, including addictions to recreational drugs, alcohol, or food.

The provider will order and interpret several blood and urine tests to rule out medical conditions that may cause depression. As an active partner in your physical health, you will arrange a sit-down with the provider to discuss the results of the tests and plan necessary corrective actions. Aside from a thorough physical examination, laboratory tests will be completed. These tests will include:

Complete Blood Count (CBC). A CBC looks at the diverse types of cells found in blood and counts how many there are. The test can check for anemia or infection that leads to fatigue and extreme tiredness even after a good night's sleep. Fatigue is associated with depression.

Thyroid Function Panel. Thyroid tests check the blood for levels of hormones produced by the thyroid gland. If the thyroid gland is under or overactive, symptoms linked to depression can result.

Creatinine and Blood Urea Nitrogen (BUN). Creatinine and BUN levels reflect how well the kidneys are working. Kidney disease can lead to symptoms like depression, but it's also essential to know if kidney function is impaired before taking antidepressants. When the kidneys are not working correctly, they do not metabolize medications properly.

Liver Function Panel. If the liver is inflamed or damaged, there are often detectable changes identified with a blood test. Liver disease can cause symptoms like depression, such as lethargy. If a person's liver isn't functioning correctly, it can indicate alcohol abuse which can cause depression. Knowing how well the liver works before taking medications is essential, as the organ's ability to metabolize drugs properly can influence how effectively the medicines work.

Fasting Blood Glucose. The amount of sugar in your blood after an overnight fast can be used to detect Type 2 Diabetes. Visit WebMD and learn the number ranges for fasting and bedtime blood sugars. Depression and untreated diabetes are linked and often co-occur. Several studies report that people with diabetes have an increased risk for depression.

Take notice if you are clinically categorized as "pre-diabetic" based on blood and urine tests. Begin checking your blood sugar at home, make necessary dietary changes, lose weight if necessary, and develop a tolerable exercise program. Avoid the too-common diabetes diagnosis through your actions and avoid the serious medical problems associated with the disease.

Type 2 Diabetes is a chronic medical nuisance. But it can often be avoided or delayed. Educate yourself on the disease and closely check your food choices, food consumption, weight, and daily activity levels to prevent its onset.

Cholesterol. Cholesterol is not linked to depression, but your HDL (good, 60+) and LDL (bad, <100) cholesterol levels affect your overall health. Blood tests can detect if you have a high cholesterol level, which increases your risk for health problems associated with plaque buildup in your arteries. There are effective medicines to correct and maintain normal cholesterol levels.

Calcium and Magnesium. Calcium and magnesium levels that are either too high or low can cause depression. However, researchers recently found that a six-week course of magnesium chloride led to a reduction in depression and anxiety symptoms. This affirms the body and mind connection.

Discuss all vitamins and supplements you are taking with your medical provider. A study published in the *Journal of the American College of Cardiology* in late 2022 by Brown University researchers reviewed nine hundred clinical trials and twenty-seven types of micronutrients and found certain supplements have the most impact on heart health. These include omega-3 fatty acids, folic acid, and the antioxidant coenzyme Q10. However, overzealous use of over-the-counter (OTC) supplements can cause medical problems, and excessive amounts of any vitamin or supplement can cause serious health problems.

Folate and Vitamin B$_{12}$. Low levels of folate or Vitamin B$_{12}$ can identify pernicious anemia, which often causes symptoms of depression. Low levels can also bring on fatigue, lethargy, confusion, and memory problems.

Vitamin D$_3$. Check the D$_3$ level, as reliable research supports the use of Vitamin D$_3$ supplements in people fifty and older. Absorption of D$_3$ is limited in those who are middle-aged and older. Consider discussing this with your provider. Spending a few minutes enjoying the sun each day is always wise.

When your blood work results are reviewed, there may be clear steps for you to take. For example, if you have low folate and B12, your medical provider may recommend taking a specific supplement. A high fasting glucose level and an A1C of six or higher can be a reason for dietary changes, cutting down or even eliminating candy bars, sugared sodas, and cakes.

Suppose you are diagnosed with hypothyroidism or Type 2 Diabetes. In these cases, you may find your depression symptoms lessening as soon as you begin treatment for the underlying conditions. Your depression could be reduced or eliminated once your medical issues are managed. You can call your family medical provider to get your comprehensive physical exam.

Avoid the crowded urgent-care centers where three or more patients are seen each hour by a rushed family nurse practitioner (NP-F) who has limited laboratory and diagnostic resources. In 2022, the average urgent-care visit in Virginia ranged from $200 to $350 out of pocket. Bypass sitting for multiple hours with those in the waiting room suffering from influenza, hacking coughs, COVID-19 symptoms, and other transmissible infectious diseases.

Avoid the hospital and medical center Emergency Department for a physical examination. Do not wait for hours bypassed by the "real" emergency victims of auto crashes, gun-shot and knife wounds, and life-threatening heart attacks. In 2022, the average cost for an Emergency Department visit- even for a limited physical examination for an insured patient- was reported to be $1,982 in Virginia. Those who were uninsured were charged an average of $2,220 out of pocket.

If you do not have a family doctor, look for a "federally qualified community health center" in your area.

These non-profit 501c3 health facilities are found across the United States in both rural and inner-city areas and supply excellent medical care regardless of your insurance status or ability to pay. They are accredited and offer excellent comprehensive care.

Because federal grant dollars primarily fund these community health centers' medical and office staff salaries and operational budgets, a sliding fee scale discount is used with all patients. Patients with limited or no financial resources enrolled in a federally qualified community health center pay as little as fifteen dollars co-pay for a comprehensive visit with a physician.

Registering and using a center is easy. Bring your financial documents (recent pay stubs, sources of income if available) when you register, and an appointment is scheduled for you.

If you are uninsured, learn if you are eligible for Medicaid. Medical social workers in these clinics will aid you with applying for and receiving coverage. Also, you can check your local county or city health department for care. There are also thousands of free clinics across the United States, and there is probably one in your city or town.

This physical exam could cost you out-of-pocket dollars. But it is an investment in your health and worth the money to see that you are physically well and have a better understanding of your health. Meet with your provider to go over the test results. Act on the medical problems found.

Your test results are usually online and sent electronically by the providing agency. You can learn more about blood and urine test results by visiting WebMD, Mayo Clinic, and similar reliable health websites. Obtain your medical information from legitimate sources and avoid websites that present testimonials on medicines, lay suggestions on cures, and any advertisements for over-the-counter potions.

Be wary of homeopathic and herbalist practitioners with their elixirs and remedies. Often the elixirs and herbal remedies delay proper diagnosis and treatment by a physician.

Chiropractors are a part of our health care delivery system. Rely on them for spinal and musculoskeletal manual adjustments which are often reported to bring pain relief. Many chiropractors now supply dietary supplements and treatments without medical school, residency, or advanced training in food and nutrition.

Rely on allopathic (MD) or osteopathic (DO) physicians trained conventionally. You can be equally comfortable if your doctor has an MD or a DO credential. Prefer those physicians with fellowship training after residency and keep board certifications in their medical specialties over the years.

Make your healthcare choices with relevant and research-based information about the advantages and disadvantages of all possible courses of treatment. Become an informed consumer of health care. Keep your blood and urine lab results for future reference and comparisons over time.

If you are prescribed medicines for your physical health problems, ask the provider about the side effects. When you pick up the medications from the pharmacy, ask for a pharmacy consultation and discuss the medicines with the pharmacist. Read the drug inserts.

Physical Examination Appointment

Date: _____Time: _____

Location: _____

Medical Provider's Name and Credentials:

_____

I will bring my insurance card and my medicines, including vitamins and other over-the-counter remedies, to my appointment. I will be rigorously honest with my medical provider.

Diagnostic Results of the physical exam:

    1. _____

    2. _____

    3. _____

Your actions with follow-up appointments and provider's referrals:

    1. _____

2. _____

3. _____

Alcohol Consumption

Even in smaller amounts, alcohol can lead to depression, problematic social functioning, reduced healthcare use, and antidepressant ineffectiveness. Alcohol use increases the risk for high-risk behaviors, suicide ideation, attempts, and completed suicides.

There is mention in the media of the benefits of limited and occasional alcoholic beverage use. However, alcohol problems are more common in depressed people than in the general population. Researchers report daily alcohol abuse leads to clinical depression and dangerous and self-destructive behaviors.

You may be drinking heavily to numb your depression. Stop drinking all alcoholic beverages if you are depressed. As an alternative, cut down. Stop or limit the consumption to just three or four drinks each week. End binge drinking sprees defined by four drinks or more per sitting.

If you think you have a problem with alcohol, you probably do.

If your family members and friends suggest that you have a problem with alcohol, you do.

Depression and alcohol abuse become a deadly combination, and consumption of alcohol inhibits your healing from depression. Clear your liquor closets and throw away the beers, wines, and distilled liquors. Rid your living space of alcoholic beverages to remove temptation.

Alcoholic Beverage Reduction and Elimination

Date: _____

Alcohol consumption specifics:

_____

How you feel about your alcohol consumption:

_____

Feelings about ceasing or cutting down on your consumption:

_____

Many people who have suffered from chronic depression have stopped drinking alcohol altogether. Consider doing this, as it may make life easier for you. When pressed by others about your alcohol abstinence, suggest that you enjoy life without alcohol or are on medications that disallow alcohol use.

Alcoholism is a family disease. It affects everyone in the family. If you are an adult child of an alcoholic or drug addict, it may be wise for you to stop drinking based on this family background, as it often leads to your own alcoholism and drug addiction.

Those who have grown up in alcoholic or addicted homes may also have undiagnosed post-traumatic stress disorder (PTSD), severe anxiety with anxiety attacks, and social phobias, which need to be treated in therapy. It is usual to have mental health co-morbidities for those who have grown up in homes with alcohol or drug addiction.

Because alcohol can be expensive, put your money to better use and into a monthly gym membership, a periodic massage, a spa day, or a frequent family dinner at an expensive restaurant. You can treat yourself and others and celebrate your life without alcohol as you work to improve your well-being.

Marijuana and Recreational Drug Use

Marijuana smoking and recreational drug use have direct connections to depression. The American Medical Association (AMA) recently reported that persons struggling with depression are much more likely to use marijuana to ease their depressive symptoms.

A spike in marijuana use is being reported after the pandemic. CDC reports that depressed people are more than twice as likely to have used pot within the last month and three times more likely to have used it daily over the past month in 2022.

Medical experts report a boom in marijuana use among depressed people. It is partly due to legalization laws across the United States and previously forced isolation and social distancing during the pandemic. However, even if marijuana is legal in your state, reduce or stop using this popular recreational drug.

If you have a medical marijuana card for medicinal use, discuss your frequency of use and its effects with your medical provider. Is marijuana use helping you with, for example, your chronic physical pain, reducing the impact of PTSD, or reducing the side effects of cancer treatment medicines?

Marijuana Use

Date: _____

Specifics of frequency per week:

_____

Notes on eliminating or cutting down use:

_____

If you are depressed, you may be using other drugs besides marijuana. You may abuse prescription or illicit drugs like OxyContin, Percocet, Valium, methadone, morphine, crack, meth, fentanyl, ecstasy, or PCP. These are dangerous and addictive substances.

If you are a regular user of opioids, discuss your use with your medical provider. You may be addicted from your use. Discuss the possibility of outpatient or residential detoxification and drug treatment programs. The United States has over fourteen thousand outpatient and residential treatment centers for alcohol and drug addictions, and a center is likely near you.

Better programs treat drug or alcohol addiction and co-occurring mental illnesses like depression, PTSD, and anxiety. When considering a treatment center, look past the glamorous TV advertisements and warm and fuzzy treatment program websites. It is essential to ask the following:

1. Are you accredited by CARF, the Joint Commission, and state regulators?

2. Do you follow the ASAM and Matrix guidelines for care?

3. Do you have an aftercare program so crucial to long-term recovery after the treatment?

Accreditation usually assures quality care. It is essential to ask about these matters in any conversations leading to admissions. This research should not be rushed. These facilities must adhere to all guidelines.

The treatment programs are for-profit and non-profit and vary in cost. A thirty-day residential stay can range from a few hundred dollars at a non-profit community facility to $60,000 at a for-profit facility.

The for-profit facilities often have private suites, room service, swimming pools, golf courses, equine therapy, weekly massages, and chef-prepared meals. While pleasant, these amenities lead to a more significant expense. Many facilities are on the beachfront, and swimming, sailing, surfing, and scuba diving are part of the treatment experience.

Most addiction treatment experts assert that these amenities are pampering and pleasant. However, the amenities add little to addiction treatment and recovery. Treatment and recovery go on with extensive education and therapy within the facility's walls.

It is essential that the facilities have qualified administrators and licensed clinical staff members. It is critical that these facilities adhere to the accreditation guidelines, which, incidentally, do not mention, for example, surfing, massage, or horseback riding.

These for-profit programs accept private insurance like Anthem, Cigna, and UnitedHealth Group. They happily accept cash for their services. For the uninsured, they accept credit card payments and offer long-term payment plans for care.

Non-profit substance abuse treatment facilities are both residential and outpatient. They are operated by federal, state, and local government agencies and accept private insurance, Medicaid, Medicare, Tricare, Veterans Affairs, and other forms of coverage.

A few non-profit programs have limited or no co-pays for residential and outpatient treatment. These programs provide excellent care without putting you or your family into debt.

After treatment, participation in an aftercare program is critical to continued recovery.

It is wisest to attend an accredited non-profit outpatient facility close to home.

Ideally, consider a facility near your home for family member involvement and recovery. Visit the facility, meet the treatment staff, and discuss the treatment program as a guest visitor before making a financial or time commitment.

Because of the expense of the proprietary centers, prospective clients and their families want assurances of treatment effectiveness. Programs now report "success rates" for those who complete the program. These numbers are usually in the high ninetieth percentiles, which should be encouraging.

However, researchers report that the programs' methods for figuring out these statistics are questionable. Those who relapse and use alcohol or drugs again often do not respond to follow-up surveys. Contacting them is difficult, especially if they have traveled across the country for residential treatment or have since moved.

Alcohol and drug addiction treatment can be life-changing. Ceasing or cutting down on your use of alcohol and drugs leads to significant improvements in your life. Your thinking is more precise, and the fog is lifted. Eliminating the substances is challenging and takes "one day at a time." But it leads to a healthier and happier life. Slips and relapses are likely through the months and years, but the wise folks keep coming back because the concepts learned in recovery treatment truly work.

For more information on residential and outpatient treatment centers, visit the local non-profit mental health agencies in your city or town for more details. Also, visit Amazon.com or the local library for literature and consider reading Syre's *Healing Your Addictions: Guide to Outpatient and Residential Treatment,* published in 2020. It provides detailed information about addiction treatment and recovery.

Recreational Drug Intake and Planned Reduction

Drug(s):

    1. _____

    2. _____

Actions taken on use and reduction with dates:

    1. _____

    2. _____

If you have been prescribed medicines for your medical conditions like hypertension, diabetes mellitus, high cholesterol, or arthritis, fill the prescriptions. Carefully read the prescription inserts for proper dosage and use and follow the directions. If you encounter adverse reactions to the prescribed medicines, call the provider's office at once and discuss the matter with the physician or registered nurse,

Tobacco Products

There is currently no cause-effect relationship between tobacco product use and depression. It is widely known that smoking and vaping tobacco products are unhealthy and expensive habits. This includes hookah smoking.

The health benefits of smoking cessation are many and are common knowledge today. Visit the CDC website (cdc.gov) if you wish to quit smoking or using other tobacco products. Your quitting may include nicotine replacement therapy.

Tobacco Reduction or Elimination

Date: _____

Smoking, vaping, chewing frequency:

_____

Efforts to reduce or eliminate:

1. _____

2. _____

Feelings about reduction or elimination:

_____

Successes: _____

Smoking, vaping, and chewing are difficult habits to break. Seek medical help from your provider. Also seek social support for your cessation. Ask your friends who have quit and are tobacco-free if it improves the quality of their lives. They will persuade you to eliminate tobacco from your life.

Visit the CDC website for comprehensive information and advice on cessation. For support in quitting, including free quit coaching, a free quit plan, free educational materials, and referrals to local resources, call 800-784-8669.

Finally, aside from the many health benefits, consider the money you save by cutting down or quitting your tobacco habit as a bonus.

Sleep Hygiene

Poor sleep is linked to depression, and you can do some things. Spend time in the sunshine during the day for Vitamin D absorption. Develop a personal sleep hygiene program so that you sleep six to eight hours each night.

Sleep hygiene involves limiting naps during the day and avoiding caffeine and nicotine close to bedtime. If you consume alcohol, avoid its consumption near bedtime. Also, briskly walk or run for fifteen minutes during the day and refrain from eating fried meats and spicy dishes and drinking caffeinated drinks near bedtime.

Establish a bedtime routine, including a warm-to-cold shower, reading a book, and listening to a meditation recording on a CD, YouTube Music, or Apple Music. You can surf YouTube for sleep-inducing recordings.

YouTube also has many recordings of Catholic Mass hymns, nighttime prayers, and rosary recitations. Enjoy the Catholic music by John Michael Talbot and Jesuit Father Bob Dufford SJ, which is calming and comforting. Their music induces sleep.

Make sure you have comfortable pillows and a firm mattress. See that your pillowcases and sheets are cozy fabrics. Consider blackout curtains and eyeshades to create a dark room. Buy a quiet tower or ceiling fan for bedroom air movement. Keep the bedroom chilly with a temperature between sixty and sixty-five degrees, where a blanket or comforter is needed for comfortable sleep.

Avoid prescription sleep medicines like Ambien and the many hypnotics available. Decline prescriptions for a nonbenzodiazepine (ex. Lunesta, Sonata) or an antidepressant (ex. Prozac, Wellbutrin) for sleep. If you continue to have sleep problems after instituting a sleep hygiene program, discuss over-the-counter sleep products like melatonin or an antihistamine with your medical provider and pharmacist.

If you live in a noisy city where the constant sounds of police cars, fire trucks, trains, and ambulance sirens keep you awake through the night, consider moving your bed away from the wall next to the street. Use white noise electronics and get inexpensive foam acoustic panels for the wall which are easily bought on Amazon.com. Purchase new pillows, colorful bed linens, and firm mattresses every few years to improve the quality of your sleep.

You may have sleep problems due to sleep apnea, a severe medical problem. Sleep apnea is a common condition where your breathing stops and restarts many times an hour while you sleep. This breathing pattern prevents your body from getting enough oxygen. Risk factors for sleep apnea include age and obesity. The illness is more common in men, and symptoms include snoring loudly and feeling tired even after a whole night's sleep.

Sleep apnea treatment involves lifestyle changes, including weight loss and using a breathing assistance device at night, such as a continuous positive airway pressure (C-PAP, Bi-Pap) machine. If left untreated for years, sleep apnea can lead to heart damage including atrial fibrillation.

With the nation's aging population increasing and escalating obesity rates, over two hundred thousand new cases of sleep apnea are diagnosed each year in the United States. Medical center diagnostic sleep laboratories are now often backlogged for months.

Sleep Hygiene Actions

Date: _____

Actions:

1. _____

2. _____

3. _____

Stress and Its Management

Stress is an accumulation of worries that causes imbalances in a person's life. Stress is an overload that throws your life out of equilibrium and often leads to depression. Stressors can involve, for example, your physical health, mental health, the quality of your relationships, finances, living environment, social environment, and career.

Paying the rent or mortgage, the utility bills, gasoline for the automobile, and putting food on the table are significant stressors for many families during this time of inflation. Other costs include phone bills, internet, cable subscriptions, and ever-rising auto and life insurance premiums.

Post-pandemic increased food prices are startling. It is no surprise that the sixty thousand food pantries across America are busy. To relieve stress, these pantries supply food so that people may feed their families. Quality foods include meats, poultry, eggs, fresh vegetables, and fruit juices. Diapers are provided to families with infants and toddlers.

How many food pantries are in your town or city? A simple internet search will inform you. City and town halls encourage the use of food pantries and act to support families struggling with food insufficiency. Also, the city and county public schools often supply free lunches for all students throughout the calendar year to ensure that the children get at least one complete meal each day.

Qualifying for food pantry foods is easy, with only a few qualifying questions. If you need help feeding yourself or your family, investigate and visit the food pantries in your community and take advantage of their offerings.

Also, homelessness is a significant stressor and is now at epidemic proportions. In cities like New York City, Los Angeles, Seattle, San Diego, and San Jose, homeless families struggle with violence, limited access to health care, unsanitary living conditions, safety issues, and exposure to severe weather. Shelters are available in cities and towns. Homelessness is a significant stressor that leads to depression in the entire family, including the children.

Recognize the signs of stress and minimize its effects on our lives. Stress makes it more challenging to reduce your depression. Some signs of stress include irritability, feeling overwhelmed, sleep disturbances, constant fatigue, significant weight gain or loss, memory problems, and anxiety attacks.

Reduce the stress in your life. Stress-reduction activities include investing time in hobbies and activities that you enjoy. These can consist of listening to your favorite music on Amazon Music or YouTube, taking a walk in a local arboretum, doing yoga and mindfulness exercises, and deep breathing while waiting at a stop light while driving in traffic. Visiting your local Starbucks Café and enjoying a hot latte or cold Frappuccino as an occasional special treat with a good friend can be relaxing.

If your church is open during the day, silence your phone, enter, light a candle, and pray for the family and loved ones who are struggling or have died, recite the traditional Catholic prayers, and be grateful for all you have. Meditate on the Crucifix and find comfort.

Spend time visiting your local public library, browse the magazine section, and review the latest best sellers. These can be a pleasant diversion for a weekend afternoon. Sit outside on a sunny day and feel the calming sun's warmth on your face. These are simple things that relieve stress.

One book you will find particularly helpful for stress reduction is *Abundance: The Inner Path to Wealth* by Deepak Chopra, MD. While the author spends time writing about wealth accumulation tactics, he discusses how each of us can become better agents of our change. He discusses stress reduction techniques and meditation and mindfulness methods that can help us focus our attention on our stability, creativity, and love for others.

Deepak Chopra's discussion about moving from emotional poverty to emotional richness is captivating. The author gives a unique view on how to move from depression to excellent mental health.

Become More Active

According to the American Heart Association, adults should ideally aim for at least one hundred fifty minutes of moderate-intensity physical activity or at least seventy-five minutes of vigorous-intensity physical activity each week. Plan for it in your schedule. If possible, exercise with a spouse, partner, or friend.

If you have a chronic medical condition or are sixty years or older, you should check with your medical provider before starting a new home or gym exercise program. Your medical provider will recommend safe exercises for you and let you know the exercises you should avoid.

Regardless of your age, gyms employ personal trainers who can advise you on safely using various exercise equipment. Do not hesitate to ask for their guidance in equipment use to avoid injury.

Exercise reduces depression while it elevates mood. Sadly, depressed people find excuses not to exercise. Often limited time is the excuse. But with over ten thousand minutes available in a week, we can carve out an hour or two. For example, spending an hour less each day visiting Facebook will give anyone ample time to exercise. Consider walking in a park as an alternative to a gym activity and doing the treadmill.

Exercise is vital because it reduces stress, prevents weight gain, boosts the immune system, and improves sleep.

Engage in physical activity with a family member or friend. Go outdoors, visit the free YouTube fitness resources online, or attend a gym fitness class. Set exercise goals and do calorie-burning chores like mowing the lawn, vacuuming, or dusting. Tailor the exercises to what you enjoy or at least tolerate.

If you do not wish to leave your house or apartment, visit YouTube and search "exercises" to see what you might like. You will be amazed at the recordings available to children, adults, and senior citizens. These recordings include music and timed walking and running in place, calisthenics, and stretching. The videos will interest people of all ages.

You can always find excuses not to exercise, and skipping your workouts is tempting. Still, health officials report that exercise is essential to physical and mental well-being after the pandemic. Exercise is an ever-important issue for those who suffer from chronic diseases like hypertension and Type 2 Diabetes. There are many reasons for exercising.

Exercise boosts the immune system. Moderate-intensity exercise has immune-boosting benefits. It helps your body fight off infections, including the coronavirus infection and its many variants that continue to evolve in 2023 and beyond.

Exercise prevents or limits weight gain. Daily aerobic exercise helps you burn calories and offsets the effects of overeating. While seeing how few calories you burn in a brisk forty-five-minute walk on the inclined treadmill is disappointing, even these few hundred calories contribute to weight loss over time. Exercise can lift your mood for the entire day.

Exercise reduces stress. Exercise helps to reduce stress levels and builds emotional resilience. It may seem mindless to run on a treadmill, even with headphones, and listen and sweat to your favorite songs. But once you have completed your miles, you walk away feeling better, and the stressful issues you may encounter are diminished.

Exercise improves your sleep. Regular exercise helps you fall asleep faster and stay asleep. It enhances the quality and depth of your sleep. Getting a good night's sleep also boosts your immune system and reduces depression.

Exercise fights your chronic illnesses. Exercise can be especially beneficial for older adults and people with chronic conditions such as diabetes, arthritis, heart disease, and even sleep apnea. Regular exercise improves balance, flexibility, strength, mobility, and cardiovascular health. Also, exercise boosts your energy levels and overall feelings of well-being.

Exercise for family fun. Exercise is an excellent opportunity for family fun. Exercising with family members can lead to heightened closeness among the family members. Consider running mini marathons together. Walks, bike rides, and living-room yoga sessions are examples of how you and your family can exercise together.

Go outdoors. Jogging, biking, and hiking can help you get much-needed fresh air. If you do not have time for a full-length outdoor exercise session, break your workouts into several ten-minute sessions. You will be surprised how quickly a few brisk walks around the block or in a park can add to complete training for the day.

Watch exercise videos. Whether you enjoy yoga, Pilates, strength training, dance, or another type of workout, chances are you will find a video that offers the activity on YouTube or Amazon.com. Additionally, many gyms and exercise studios now provide on-demand virtual fitness classes.

Take classes. Sign up for fitness classes in the pool or gym. Take advantage of training sessions with a personal trainer. Some personal trainers offer private sessions customized to your unique needs, schedule, and preferences. Plus, training sessions allow you to interact with another person in fun ways. Classes and training sessions may be just the motivation you need to keep up with your fitness regime several times weekly.

Those group fitness classes for Pilates, aqua aerobics, balance, and yoga provide opportunities to befriend others in the classes. Friendships are often created from conversations before and after classes, and these classes are a valuable way to connect with others in a healthy environment.

Let us challenge ourselves. You can set exercise goals, such as routinely doing Pilates three days per week or beating your best 5K time. Meeting or exceeding your challenges is a boost to your self-esteem. Your confidence in your physical health improves.

Tackle calorie-burning chores. Working in the garden or cleaning the garage or storage closet can supply excellent opportunities to build muscle and burn calories. In addition to the sense of accomplishment you feel after the chores, completing these tasks yields the benefits of a more beautiful garden and cleaner household.

A Healthier Diet

Our typical American supermarket seduces the shopper with a wide selection of foods that can make us sick, especially when consumed in excess. Examples include the jumbo bags of potato chips, cases of sugared sodas, boxes of donuts, bags of candy, and quarts of ice cream that fill the shoppers' baskets.

Aside from wreaking havoc on our bodies, they are expensive investments in disease. Unsurprisingly, resulting from our diets, Americans are burdened with Type 2 Diabetes, a range of heart diseases, and obesity. However, you have control over your food choices and eating habits.

There is no specific diet proven to relieve depression in the medical literature. However, certain foods ease your symptoms and put you in a better mood. In addition, a healthy diet helps as part of your overall improved lifestyle.

We may find comfort in discussing our "fat" genes and heredity as obesity and chronic illnesses run in families. But what we put into our mouths daily is one of the most significant predictors of our weight and overall physical and mental health.

Besides mood swings, our diets influence our physical appearance and the development of chronic diseases like obesity, diabetes, heart disease, and cancer. There are, however, professionals who can help. A registered dietician (RD) in a clinic or hospital can educate you.

Registered Dieticians (RD) are experts in diet and food intake and can guide you in better control of your food consumption and weight loss.

For example, RDs promote eating complex carbs. Whole grains are better than simple carbs found in cakes and cookies. Fruits, vegetables, and legumes have healthy carbs and fiber. Carbohydrates are linked to the mood-boosting brain chemical serotonin, which is the crucial hormone that stabilizes your mood, feelings of well-being, and happiness. Serotonin influences your entire body and helps with sleep and digestion.

Choose your carbs wisely. As tasty as they are, sugary foods, boxes of candy, and bags of chips are poor food choices. Choose apples, oranges, bananas, and other fruit instead. Consider munching on carrots as an alternative to a giant Snickers bar or a sleeve of stuffed Oreo cookies. Choose flavored club soda as an alternative to a Big Gulp Coke or large Pepsi.

Medicare Part B and some private insurance carriers fully cover dietary consultations with Registered Dieticians (RD) if the person has Type 2 Diabetes. It is preventive medicine. Make an appointment and meet for an hour with an RD every two weeks for three months at the local clinic or hospital. Remember that weight loss is a marathon. Buy an accurate weight scale and weigh yourself weekly.

Turkey, tuna, and chicken contain protein and have an amino acid called tryptophan which helps you make serotonin. Eat something with protein a few times a day, especially when you need to clear your mind and boost your energy level. Reliable sources of healthy proteins include beans and peas, fish, chicken, low-fat cheese, milk, soy products, and yogurt.

While a radical concept for most in American society, distinguished physicians today advocate eliminating refined sugar from the diet. Their research and recommendations are published in the top-tier medical and nutrition journals in the United States and Europe. Their arguments are research-based and persuasive as they discuss skyrocketing Type 2 Diabetes rates, morbid obesity rates, cardiovascular disease, and multiple other maladies.

A kinder and gentler approach is to cut down on refined sugar products like sugared sodas, fruit juices, cakes, and candy. When food shopping, go first to the store produce section and seek out the green leafy vegetables. Read the food labels of canned goods for fructose and salt content. Learn to eat green leafy vegetable salads and use simple low calorie dressings on a regular basis.

Dietary Changes

1._____ Date:_____

2._____ Date:_____

3. _____ Date:_____

Weight:_____ Date:_____

Weight:_____ Date:_____

Vitamin B Complex. There is a link between B vitamin levels and depression. However, researchers need to find out which way the influence goes. Do poor nutrient levels lead to depression? Or does depression lead people to eat poorly? B vitamins are found in all lean and low-fat animal products, such as fish and low-fat dairy products. You can vary your diet with, for example, salmon or flounder. Use turmeric in your cooking and consume limited dark chocolate and yogurt.

Limit your caffeine intake. You do not need to stop all caffeine intake. But limit the double and triple espressos, multiple cups of coffee, energy drinks, and caffeine-laden colas. There is no clear link between caffeine intake and depression, but caffeine intake and depression are linked to people who are sensitive to the effects of caffeine or consume too much of it.

Limit all forms of caffeine, including chocolate, in the evenings. Limiting caffeine improves sleep. Excessive caffeine intake causes sleep problems that affect your mood. For most, caffeine makes it harder to fall asleep and remain asleep. A lack of sleep worsens depression. You may need to limit caffeine to the morning or stop drinking caffeinated beverages altogether to avoid sleep problems. An alternative is hot or iced green tea.

Reduce your consumption of energy drinks like Red Bull®, Monster®, and energy shots like Red Line® and Energy Shot®. The considerable amounts of caffeine in these drinks can cause increased blood pressure and a greater heart rate, while the other drink ingredients can lead to abnormal heart rhythms, aneurysms, and, on rare occasions, unexpected heart attacks.

These products are marketed as "harmless," but they are not. Also, they are expensive, and it is better to invest your dollars in bottles of water or noncaloric club soda.

Depression and anxiety often co-occur, and caffeine and energy drinks can worsen anxiety. If you stop abruptly with the caffeine and energy drinks, your depression may worsen. If you regularly drink caffeinated beverages, quitting can cause a further depressed mood until your body adjusts. Abruptly stopping can also cause other signs and symptoms of depression, such as fatigue and irritability. Wean off caffeine products slowly over weeks to avoid adverse reactions.

Relationships

An essential activity for depression reduction is recognizing and affirming your healthy relationships. Also, consider developing new healthy relationships. Your healthy and positive relationships are crucial to lifting you from your depression.

Cheerful, caring, and helping relationships boost mood and help diminish your depression.

Think about the people around you. These include your spouse or partner, close friends, roommates, housemates, coworkers, acquaintances, and others you interact with regularly. Each person influences your mental health. You want to feel loved and supported by those around you, and in healing from depression, you seek to surround yourself with affirming and encouraging people as much as possible.

Gain from positive personal relationships with people who look through the lenses of love, joy, beauty, and hope for you to thrive. Affirm that your warm and personal relationships transcend your job title, size of your home, salary, or disposable income.

Reflect on your relationships. Do you feel good about the people in your life? It is time to look honestly at your current relationships to determine whether they help or hurt you. You may need to end some of your relationships, strengthen others, and find new ones.

You want to be in relationships that support you, help you grow, and positively contribute to your life. Find people who enjoy their lives and care about you and others. This can be transformational for you.

Seek kindness, honesty, caring, support, and authenticity in your relationships. Pursue these qualities in others. But more importantly, share these qualities with those close to you. Two other qualities critical to good relationships are respect and the ability to listen.

Search for the optimists in your social circle. They look through the lens of hope. Optimists are reported to be more consistent in their healthy habits. Researchers say that optimists sleep better and eat more vegetables than pessimists. As you spend time with optimists, try to emulate them as they see the brighter side of life.

The damaging words "should have" and "could have" that bring people down are usually not found in the lexicon of optimists. Optimists may have many life regrets, but they have learned to move past them to pursue a brighter present and future.

Your Relationships

Name: _____

Assessment: _____

A way to improve the relationship:

_____

Name: _____

Assessment: _____

A way to improve the relationship:

_____

Name: _____

Assessment: _____

A way to improve the relationship:

_____

Golden Rule Adherence

The Golden Rule guides us to choose for others what we would choose for ourselves. The Golden Rule is often described as "putting ourselves in someone else's shoes," or 'Doing unto others as we would have them do unto ourselves."

The viewpoint held in the Golden Rule is noted in all the major world religions and cultures; it is a moral truth.

The Golden Rule is mentioned in the *Bible's* Book of Luke, Chapter 7, but also by Pope Francis in a speech to the U.S. Joint Session of Congress in 2014. He mentioned his concern for America's homeless, hungry, refugee population, and care for the unborn and weakened elderly.

The pope also mentioned three sons and a daughter of America who had dreams. They were Lincoln with liberty; Martin Luther King, Jr, with liberty in plurality and equality; Dorothy Day with social justice and the rights of persons; and Trappist monk Thomas

Merton, the distinguished author who wrote about prayer life and openness to God.

The Golden Rule is also mentioned in the National Library of Medicine in publications related to medical and nursing care delivery. The rule is relevant to direct medical care delivery, administration of clinical services, and medical and staff continuing education programming.

This rule leads us to completing acts of kindness, caring, and altruism that go beyond "business as usual." As such, this ethic has universal appeal and helps guide our behaviors toward the welfare of others.

Consider your actions and apply the Golden Rule in your relationships with family members, church members, colleagues, and strangers.

Golden Rule Application

What are three specific ways that I may strengthen my actions using the Golden Rule?

1. _____

2. _____

3. _____

4. _____

Sensory Awareness and Engagement

You have five senses and they influence how you feel. Mindfully using these five senses can boost your mood and, at the same time, reduce your depression. Use your senses to feel better. Activities using the senses that can positively influence your mood include:

Hearing. Listen to soothing music favorites, whether it is country music, classical music, jazz, or the blues. You may have a favorite music album you enjoy hearing. You may have a memorable song from a C.D. or a vinyl album that you associate with happy moments from decades ago. Alternatively, visit a park and listen to the birds sing in the spring and summer.

Physical touch. Touch is a mighty comforter. Physical touch increases your levels of dopamine and serotonin, two neurotransmitters that help regulate your mood and relieve stress and anxiety. Dopamine also regulates the pleasure center in your brain, which can offset feelings of depression and anxiety.

Hugging does matter. Hug your family members and close friends. When you engage in pleasant touch like a hug, your brain releases a hormone called oxytocin. This makes you feel good and strengthens emotional and social bonds while lowering anxiety.

Also, spend time in a sauna and whirlpool at the gym. Take a long, high-pressure hot-then-freezing cold shower. Get an occasional therapeutic massage that will improve your mood and relieve aches and pains.

Smell. Aromas from the kitchen, a restaurant, or an outdoor location near a lawn and garden can be pleasurable. The smells can include, for example, cooked bacon, freshly baked bread, coffee, or newly cut grass. It can be the salty air from the ocean waves breaking on a shoreline.

Scents can positively affect how you feel as you associate them with moments during the holidays and festivities. Pleasant aromas can also include calming lavender and rose oil.

Sights. Visit a local community nursery or flower garden to admire the natural beauty. Travel to see the leaves change in the fall or the ocean to watch the waves break. Visit Boston's aquarium or NYC's Guggenheim to view your favorite aqua life, paintings, and sculptures. Climb the Statue of Liberty. Ride the cable cars in San Francisco. Visit the Grand Canyon and the Outer Banks.

It is time to think with an adventurous spirit. Travel internationally and visit the Vatican's Saint Peter's Cathedral, the Pieta, and the Sistine Chapel. Climb the Eiffel Tower, the Great Wall, and even Mount Kilimanjaro. If you are careful in your planning, you can still travel internationally on a limited budget; find inexpensive round-trip flights, use only public transport, stay in youth or elder hostels, and dine in the local marketplaces enjoying the local cuisine.

Traveling can be both thrilling and life-changing. It will diminish your depression. National and international travel gets you out of yourself to focus on the adventure of experiencing exciting new and exotic places and all they have to offer. Travel with family members to share memorable experiences.

Taste. To enhance your dishes and mood, flavor your foods with herbs and spices like cinnamon, bay leaves, curry, berbere, and mint. Your town may have a variety of ethnic restaurants. Savor dishes from Ethiopia, El Salvador, and Vietnam. Enjoy a piece of rich, dark, imported chocolate. Visit your local town ethnic bakeries and purchase tasty Mexican, Italian, or French pastries as special treats for you and your family members to enjoy.

Too often, we all take our senses for granted. Recognize the joys that your senses can bring to you. Appreciating them leads to your improved quality of life.

Write about specific engagements with your senses:

Hearing: _____

Physical touch: _____

Smell: _____

Sights: _____

Taste: _____

Virtues and Character Strengths

Discover the positive qualities within yourself. Learn about the six virtues and twenty-four-character strengths that each of us has regardless of our mental health status.

While you will learn about positive psychology later in *Healing Your Depression: A Catholic Perspective, 2ⁿᵈ Ed.,* this part discusses learning more about ourselves. Each of us has twenty-four strengths reported by the VIA Institute on Character found in Cincinnati, which you are encouraged to visit on the internet. These include:

Virtue of Wisdom and Its Character Strengths

- Creativity: thinking of novel and productive ways to do things

- Curiosity: openness to experiencing and taking an interest in ongoing experiences

- Open-mindedness: thinking things through and examining them from all sides

- Love of learning: mastering new skills and bodies of knowledge

- Perspective: supplying wise counsel to ourselves and others

Virtue of Temperance and Its Character Strengths

- Forgiveness and mercy: forgiving those who have hurt us or done us wrong; accepting the shortcomings of others; giving others and ourselves a second chance; not being vengeful

- Humility and modesty: letting our accomplishments speak for themselves; not regarding ourselves as superior to others; not bragging or boasting

- Prudence: being careful about our life choices; not taking undue risks, not doing things that we might later regret

- Self-regulation: regulating what we feel and do; being disciplined, controlling ourselves in behavior and appetite

Virtue of Courage and Its Character Strengths

- Bravery: accepting challenges and not withdrawing from threats or pain

- Perseverance: finishing what we start and persisting during action despite the obstacles we meet

- Integrity: speaking the truth and presenting ourselves in a genuine and authentic manner

- Vitality and zest: approaching our lives with excitement, energy, and hope; being passionate as we complete our responsibilities

Virtue of Humanity and Its Character Strengths

- Love: valuing our close relationships with others, particularly those in which caring and sharing are reciprocated; being emotionally close to people

- Kindness: doing virtuous deeds for others; helping others; caring for family, friends, and strangers

- Social intelligence: being aware of the motivations and feelings of others; knowing what to do to fit into different social situations; understanding what makes other people tick

Virtue of Justice and its Character Strengths

- Citizenship and teamwork: working effectively as a member of a group; being loyal to a group; doing our share in a group

- Fairness: treating all persons in the same way according to the notions of fairness and justice; not allowing our personal feelings, biases, or prejudices lead to decisions about others; giving everyone a fair chance

- Leadership: encouraging a group of which we are a member to get things done and, at the same time, maintaining good relations within the group; organizing group activities and seeing them completed; collaborating with people to achieve the mission

Virtue of Transcendence and Its Character Strengths

- Appreciation of beauty and excellence: appreciating beauty, excellence, or skilled performances in all venues of life, from nature to the fine arts, to math, to the sciences

- Gratitude: being aware of and thankful for the good things in our lives; taking time to express thanks for all we have

- Hope and optimism: expecting the best in the future and working to achieve it; believing that good things will occur in the future

- Humor: laughing and appreciating the humor in life; bringing smiles to others; seeing the lighter sides of life

- Spirituality: having belief in a higher power in our lives; shaping our conduct and belief systems to provide comfort to ourselves and others

Your Character Strengths

One of the ways to overcome depression and increase happiness is to learn more about the many strengths you have today. Regardless of how depressed you have become, you possess character strengths that you can recognize, celebrate, and use.

Visit the VIA Institute on Character on the internet. Take the *Values in Action Inventory,* composed of 240-items. The results are immediately delivered. It is uplifting to read the results about your character strengths. Print or file your results. You can retake the survey every six months to see if there are any changes in your signature character strengths.

You can complete the inventory in less than forty minutes. Since 2001, over four hundred thousand people have completed the survey. Participants are instructed to answer each item in the inventory using a Likert scale. It is simple yet informative.

Scored reports are delivered to you after the survey. Feedback is provided for your strengths. The results rank your strengths from one to twenty-five, with the top five strengths considered your "signature character strengths." You can post the list of your character strengths on your refrigerator door for frequent viewing and self-affirmation.

Your character strengths matter. They especially matter when you are feeling depressed. When things are going poorly, you can review your character strengths to balance the struggles you face and shift your focus from negative to positive.

You can use your character strengths to help you see what is best in you and others. Thinking about your character strengths enables you to avoid becoming overly critical of yourself by thinking about your strengths rather than what is wrong with you.

By studying your character strengths, you focus on your positive qualities. You can link your positive strengths with positive feelings and improve your relationships with your spouse, partner, and family members. This knowledge can lead to greater self-acceptance because it focuses on the positive.

Memorize your five signature character strengths and consciously think about them during your waking hours. Apply your strengths to reduce stress and experience fewer physical ailments. Apply your signature character strengths to cope with the occasional traumatic situation.

Positive Psychology Center

The University of Pennsylvania, located in Philadelphia, has a Positive Psychology Center and a happiness website. Visit the website. It provides free resources to learn about positive psychology through readings, videos, research findings, conferences, and questionnaires with feedback.

There is no charge to use this helpful and uplifting website. It has a rich array of learning and teaching materials. These useful questionnaires only require a simple registration with a username and password.

Positive psychology is the scientific study of the strengths and virtues that enable individuals, families, workgroups, and communities to thrive. This field is founded on the belief that we want to lead meaningful and fulfilling lives, cultivate what is best within ourselves, and enhance our work experiences, love, and play. Remember that it is not what is wrong with you. It is what is strong with you.

Chapter Activity: Complete the character strengths survey on the VIA Character website and list your five signature character strengths. Briefly describe a situation within the last week that you demonstrated your use of each of these strengths.

Signature Character Strengths/Demonstration

1. _____

2. _____

3. _____

4. _____

5. _____

After completing the VIA survey and receiving your report, reflect on the findings. Do not file the document away but print it and keep the report handy and readily available for you to review periodically.

Be mindful of your character strengths daily. In your daily conversations with others, identify how you demonstrate your signature and other character strengths.

If your three top signature character strengths are, for example, gratitude, kindness, and forgiveness, how do you apply these strengths in your daily activities and interactions with others? Be specific:

1. _____

2. _____

3. _____

Consider the worn cliché and simple truth, "Practice makes perfect." You improve whatever you practice, whether with your thinking, words, or actions. These practices involve the twenty-four character strengths associated with your thought processes, eating and drinking habits, how you invest your time, exercising or not exercising, and even mass attendance and participation in the sacraments. They become your habits. Our routines bring us comfort.

But habits can change. Your actions and words can lead you to either improve or diminish your personal strengths and the quality of your life. Remember that what you think and do are choices you make just as the habits you perpetuate daily are also choices.

Chapter 4

The Therapist Search

Great and glorious God, and Thou Lord Jesus, I pray you to shed your light into the darkness of my mind. Be fond of me, Lord, so that in all things I may act only by Thy holy will.
Saint Francis of Assisi

Find the Right Therapist

Finding a therapist for yourself can be daunting and a bit frightening. As you search, pray to Jesus for His guidance in finding a therapist to help bring light into the darkness you are experiencing with your depression.

The best practical advice in your search is "caveat emptor," translated as "Let the buyer beware." Do not rush through the process even if you are suffering from debilitating depression.

This search is a time to be patient and cautious. Just as you search and carefully select a primary care provider, a dentist, or even a professor for a college course, put an organized effort into researching and finding the right therapist to meet your mental health needs.

Call on the Holy Spirit for His gifts of wisdom and knowledge in your search for the right therapist.

As you search for a therapist, you discover a wide diversity in credentials and qualifications among those working in the field. An easy method is to simply browser search "therapist in the area," and dozens of attractive therapist websites pop up offering telehealth and in-person appointments. It is intimidating and can even be overwhelming. While easy and fast, this search strategy is not recommended.

Local Mental Health Agencies

Search and find the mental health agencies and clinical group practices in your town or city. These agencies include community services boards, community counseling centers, and counseling and psychology groups affiliated with a hospital or medical center.

Travel to and visit these community agencies. Study their websites. For example, you might browser search "community services board." Do not be sidetracked or diverted by the inviting websites of the national proprietary agencies looking for your business. Be aware of website placements by effective search engine optimization (SEO). Bypass the "AD" advertised agencies and therapists; looking at the agency URLs is essential.

Searching the established agencies gives you assurance of therapist vetting with credentials review and convenience of ancillary services. For example, if the therapist is contracted and employed at a community services board or a community counseling center, the therapist has undergone vetting before employment to confirm that they are suitable for an appointment with the agency.

Their educational background, credentials, license, and earlier employment history have been verified. Employment references have been checked. An FBI and state background check have been completed. Those who have passed the employment muster in these agencies are more likely to be qualified.

A local established mental health agency like a community services board is more likely to have several services, including an accommodating building, a case manager, a business office manager to manage appointments and insurance billing, and a variety of mental health providers.

These agencies are recognized in the community as mental health services providers and often have ancillary emergency services, crisis stabilization and housing, a 24/7 local hotline, psychosocial rehabilitation, and accredited substance use disorder services.

Seek a therapist within the selected agency. Like other states, Virginia's established, mainstream, and recognized credentials include M.D., Doctor of Medicine (allopathic medicine), D.O., Doctor of Osteopathy (osteopathic medicine), Ph.D., Doctor of Philosophy (focus: clinical psychology), Psy.D., Doctor of Psychology (clinical practice), LCSW, Licensed Clinical Social Worker, LMFT, Licensed Marriage and Family Therapist, and LPC, Licensed Professional Counselor.

There are other credentials that therapists earn and present on their websites, including CTS, MSCP, MAC, and EMDR, and you may browser search each to see what they are. Some, for example, specialize in trauma and addictions. Rely on professionals with established and mainstream credentials with licensure in mental health.

The more recognized mainstream credentials represent years of graduate classroom study and a supervised internship or fellowship. The therapists have earned medical or graduate degrees from accredited educational institutions.

You would probably prefer a therapist who has trained for two or more years in a post-baccalaureate graduate school at a distinguished university rather than a therapist from a for-profit unaccredited college with abbreviated exclusively online training.

It is reasonable to ask about their credentials, including licensure. You might wish to investigate their programs and universities before engaging in therapy with anyone—education matters.

For those who prefer not to use an agency or do not have access to a community services board, a counseling center in the community, or a behavioral health outpatient practice affiliated with a medical center or hospital, there are other ways to find and choose a therapist.

Private Practice Search Methods

Suggestions for finding a therapist who will meet your specific needs in the community or online are offered. These suggestions range from asking close friends to using the internet.

Ask a good friend. You will be surprised who is now in mental health therapy in post-pandemic America. Ask close friends if they can recommend a therapist. You may ask if their therapist is helpful. Are your friends feeling better because of the therapy? Does the therapist use a particular modality? Ask about the ease of getting scheduled appointments. Can your friends contact the therapist in emergencies? Does the therapist accept insurance? How much does the therapist charge?

Are your friends seeing a psychiatrist or psychiatric nurse practitioner? Ask about the quality of the visits and the effectiveness of medications prescribed. How are the prescription and the provider helpful in reducing their depression? Is getting a prescription renewal easy? Do they supply samples for the more expensive psychotropics?

Primary care *providers.* Ask your medical provider if they know a therapist who can help you with your depression. Explain that you are interested in talk therapy. Ask about therapists and not only those who prescribe psychotropic medicines. Your preference is to engage in talk therapy and not simply take psychotropic medications unless necessary.

At the mention of depression in an office visit, primary care providers often offer an antidepressant prescription for depression and offer to work with you. Politely decline the medication and office therapy.

Primary care providers, especially board-certified family physicians, are a critical facet of the nation's primary care delivery system but do not have the time or expertise to conduct lengthy talk therapy sessions in their busy practices. Like psychiatrists, they often see three scheduled patients each hour. The waiting rooms are usually crowded, and they are pressed for time.

Shop online. You can shop online for a private therapist in your area. *Psychology Today* has a website with thousands of mental health providers who market their practices. Visit the *Psychology Today* website, include your zip code, and dozens of local therapists with their photos and bios pop up. Do not be overwhelmed by the academic degrees or descriptions of their clinical skills.

Psychology Today's website content is like Facebook and sales and services list platforms. Be careful and do not rush. Call and talk with them before making your first appointment. Ask lots of questions.

Visit their private office if they are local. See them for an intake in person or by a Zoom-type connection. And remember, if you are not entirely comfortable with the therapist's intake, do not return. You will be billed for the visit. Pay the bill as a facet of your search for the right therapist.

College and University Counseling Centers

Colleges and universities are responsible for the mental health of their students and providing mental health services. A December 2020 survey conducted by the American Council of Education (ACE) revealed that sixty-eight percent of university presidents surveyed stated that the mental health of their students was one of the most pressing issues facing their offices.

The American Psychological Association (APA) recently reported on collegiate mental health concerns. Fifty-eight percent of college presidents "would hire additional clinical staff members for their counseling centers if financially possible."

Campus counseling centers have multiple responsibilities. They are expected to meet the specific needs of the students, which include:

Improved student academic performance. Mental illness affects academic performance and the success of students. Poor mental health contributes to a lack of motivation, problems focusing on classroom work, and failing grades. Counseling services can improve academic performance through prompt and effective service delivery.

Prevent suicide attempts and suicide. College students are a vulnerable population for suicide attempts and completions. A report from CDC recently reported that one in every four college students contemplated suicide in the last thirty days. Campus counseling centers need to promote suicide prevention, educate the entire campus community- including students, staff, and faculty- on ways to help those who are considering the act, and teach all to help those who are struggling. From a national demographic standpoint, those aged eighteen to twenty-four are a particularly vulnerable population for suicide completion.

Educate and encourage student mental well-being in post-pandemic America. The wide variety of mental illnesses cannot be resolved with the traditional semester single, three- or even six-session counseling service alone. More is needed and often requested by students. Active Minds, Inc., which strongly supports positive psychology concepts on campuses, is a national non-profit organization supporting mental health awareness and education for young adults, and they report that thirty-nine percent of students struggle with a significant mental health issue while in college. Students need to be provided with the tools to manage their mental and emotional well-being to create a supportive campus culture where mental illness can be discussed openly. Administrators, faculty, and staff members must be educated about campus mental health and illness and how to respond.

Retain students. The National Alliance on Mental Illness (NAMI) reports that sixty-four percent of students who drop out of college do so because of a mental illness. Counseling center services and education can have an impact on improved retention. NAMI also reports that sixty-three percent of students interviewed stated that effective counseling services led to their remaining in school. Otherwise, colleges and universities risk declining graduation rates, enrollment, and student success.

Expectations are growing. Prospective college and university students and their parents are now placing a higher priority on the mental health services provided in their school selection. Crisis intervention and in-person and virtual counseling services are considered essential services by parents. More is desired by students and their parents.

Campus counseling centers are expected to adhere to clinical guidelines for the students they serve. These centers are expected to provide a set range of services in affiliation with local hospitals, medical centers, and police and sheriff departments. The guidelines are created in response to the center's mission, the knowledge, skills, and experience of its clinical staff, and the resources available to carry out its objectives.

New life experiences challenge today's students on campus. Students are afforded new freedoms, flexible school and work schedules, residence options, choices in course work, and meeting and spending time with a diverse population of students, faculty, and staff, often for the first time. Students are sometimes surprised by the accelerated academic rigors of coursework inside the classroom.

Adjustments to college can be complex, with life transitions related to gender identity and behavior, spiritual beliefs, and alcohol and drug use. Most are now away from their parents in a new geographic location. In combination, these transitions can lead a student to experience:

- Depression

- Anxiety (generalized and social)

- Relationship challenges with romance, roommates, and family

- Feeling of anger, loneliness, fear, and guilt

- Body image concerns

Furthermore, the student's family of origin is often a source of mental illness. It is estimated that one in every ten college students will come from a home with alcoholism and other drug addictions, emotional and physical violence, and family traumas that they have yet to process.

Some students arrive on campus diagnosed with one or more mood disorders. They are taking psychotropic prescriptions for their anxiety or depression and have been accustomed to ongoing weekly or biweekly intensive therapy at home.

However, expecting a college or university counseling center to provide immediate, comprehensive, and individually tailored mental health services to every student requesting these services is like asking a lone swabbie to take a 15-foot sailboat from the ports of Baltimore, USA, to Brighton, England. It is unreasonable.

College counseling centers try to maximize their assigned human and financial resources to meet as many students' mental health needs as possible. As professionals in the field of collegiate mental health, administrators and clinical staff members are committed to providing emergency mental health services, walk-in crisis intervention, and an assessment to determine the best treatment options.

These counseling centers provide individual therapy, group therapy, educational workshops, and campus-wide events. Many centers also offer couples therapy. But, because of the high demand and number of students seeking care, there are limits to the number of therapy sessions and individualized services centers can provide. Students who are distressed and often overwhelmed will complain privately and in the media about inadequate service delivery.

Counseling centers offer a wide array of self-help and mutual support mental health activities to relieve symptoms of stress, depression, and anxiety. These activities can range from campus mental health awareness weeks to offering easily accessible online educational tools to manage the mental health challenges of college life.

Forward-thinking campus counseling centers are now embracing the Positive Psychology concepts mentioned in Chapter 5 of Healing Your Depression: A Catholic Perspective, 2nd Ed. For example, the concepts can reduce the stress that leads to sleep difficulties, fatigue, a lack of motivation, excessive worry, irritability, and digestive problems.

By encouraging looking at each student's character strengths and applying the PERMA Model, the student's quality of life can improve. Campus religious organizations can also play a key role in strengthening students' mental health.

Campus counseling centers should align with the religious organizations on campus. These organizations can include, for example, the Catholic Newman Center, Baptist Student Union, and Hillel Society.

A wealth of research indicates that campus religious organizations assist students with personal adjustment and developmental challenges in higher education. These organizations serve as forums for religious services, friendship building, race and values dialogue, individual problem-solving, and campus service.

Campus priests, pastors, rabbis, imams, and other spiritual leaders can be effective sources of counseling, guidance, and direction for students struggling with life's choices away from home. These spiritual leaders are an essential thread in the fabric of campus life for students, faculty, and staff.

Students may be serviced by the college or university counseling center but also referred to community mental health agencies for additional long-term specialized care. Assistance is usually provided to help students secure referrals outside the counseling center and in the community at private and non-profit mental health group practices, hospitals, and medical centers.

In rare instances, students may suffer severe and overwhelming mental illness that requires psychiatric in-patient care followed by intensive outpatient daycare. These students are advised to take a school leave of absence and return home for comprehensive care. They can return to school when they are feeling better.

Teletherapy

The coronavirus pandemic changed how mental health services were delivered between 2018 and 2021. Fear of the coronavirus infection, the need for social distancing, and quarantining led to teletherapy as a service norm. Telephone consultations and Zoom-type platforms were used for therapy.

It has become the preferred method for conducting therapy among many clinicians today because of its convenience, increased client capacity, lower overhead in providing services, and ease of seeing clients without geographic boundaries.

There are benefits to teletherapy. You may be housebound, wish to avoid dealing with transportation issues, or prefer the comfort of your home. There is ease and convenience in sitting in a bedroom or home office and talking with a therapist on the screen.

However, there are also limitations. For instance, it may be more difficult to ensure privacy and confidentiality for both the client and the provider. Furthermore, technological issues may be a barrier as only some have a laptop with a decent camera and speaker system and access to steady high-speed internet. Not everyone is tech-savvy. For those who have privacy, possess the technology, are tech-savvy, and have reliable internet access, telehealth technology increases access to mental health care.

You may wish to lean towards in-person sessions in an agency's office. Besides heightened interpersonal interactions with the therapist, agencies are pleasant to visit, provide private therapy offices, and usually have comfortable waiting rooms and ample parking. You have ready access to the business office with scheduling and billing questions. Agencies also have 24/7 emergency access for mental health crises with telephone access to a therapist on call.

You learn from experience what is most comfortable and effective for you in the therapeutic milieu.

In your search, study the agency's website contents. If you are confident about the agency, providers, and services offered, make an appointment to visit the agency. Meet the office staff and complete the paperwork including medical history and insurance forms. If you are health insured, bring your insurance cards and ask the agency business office personnel about therapy coverage costs and co-pays.

Most local and state mental health agencies hold a 501c3 IRS letter indicating non-profit status. They receive funds from client insurance reimbursement, the city, county, state, and often United Way. Some non-profit agencies secure federal, state, and foundation grant funds for value-added mental health services.

If you are uninsured, ask about the sliding fee scale discount rate before you make an appointment. Your session costs may be as low as five dollars a session. This starkly contrasts with therapists in private practice who charge two hundred dollars an hour, are out of network, and do not accept your health insurance for services.

You learn that these independent solo practitioners request payment by cash, credit card, a bank transfer at the time of service. You are looking for the right fit in your therapeutic relationship, given the financial requirements associated with care.

Keep the therapist's contact information and financial records of all expenses associated with your mental health care for budgeting purposes and end-of-year tax declarations.

Biases and Preferences

In selecting a therapist, recognize that you have biases and preferences. If you speak English as your second or third language, request a therapist who is fluent in your language. You may prefer a woman or a man as your therapist. You may be more comfortable with someone younger or older. If you are an African American, you may wish for the same.

Personal appearance and dress codes are changing in the 2020 decade. You may wonder about the woman therapist's radiant pink hair wearing tattered blue jeans, or the men's multiple earrings, straggly ponytails, or t-shirts. Inked hands, wrists, arms, and necks may or may not put you off. Be flexible, accept, and accommodate your therapist's appearance. But it is also important to be comfortable with the person with whom you will be spend many hours.

Human sexuality and sexual orientation do matter in therapy. If you belong to the LBGTQ+ or similar vulnerable community, ask for a therapist with training and experience with these communities. Advise the agency of your preferences before you are assigned a therapist and attend your first therapy session for the best fit.

Advocate for your mental health healing and services. Even with a small co-pay, you are the paying customer. Therapy is expensive, and whether you or your insurance company is paying, you should expect ongoing quality care from a capable therapist with whom you are comfortable.

Engaging with a mental health professional, whether a licensed therapist or another provider, involves "continuity of care." Continuity of care is the process by which you and your therapist or another provider cooperatively engage in ongoing and consistent care toward the shared goal of high-quality therapy and healing. It involves establishing a relationship over time and focusing on you, your depression, and getting better.

Psychiatrists

Psychiatrists are mental health experts. They are allopathic or osteopathic physicians trained in caring for the comprehensive needs of those with mental illnesses. Their efforts usually consist of diagnosing, treatment planning, and prescribing psychotropic medications. These medicines are administered to children, teens, adults, and seniors to manage depression, anxiety, psychological distress, insomnia, and other disorders.

These clinicians prescribe psychotropics to manage your behavioral and psychiatric symptoms. Fortunately, there is often symptom relief for many.

Learning about the available psychotropics can be overwhelming. In 2022, and according to the National Institute of Health (NIH), the most popularly prescribed antidepressants were the selective serotonin reuptake inhibitors (SSRIs), a classification of antidepressants.

These popular SSRIs include Celexa, Lexapro, Prozac, Sarafem, Symbyax, Luvox, Luvox, Luvox CR, Paxil, Paxil CR, Pexeva, Viibryd, and Zoloft. Zoloft was the number one prescribed antidepressant. They vary significantly in cost and side effects; some are available in cheaper generics and others not.

To a lesser extent, a patient may also be prescribed other psychotropics. These include Abilify, Seroquel, Xanax, Ativan, Buspar, Visterol, and Propranolol.

Visit the Mayo Clinic website for a comprehensive discussion on antidepressants and antianxiety medicines.

SSRIs also treat pain and other conditions besides depression and anxiety disorders. These other disorders include premenstrual syndrome (PMS), fibromyalgia, and irritable bowel syndrome (IBS). Additionally, SSRIs are effective in treating obsessive–compulsive and panic disorders, social phobias, and eating disorders.

The vast list of available antidepressants expands annually. New ones are approved and placed on the market yearly after extensive research and Food and Drug Administration (FDA) approval.

Those who rely on psychiatrists for antidepressant medicines learn that the prescribing choices will vary among psychiatrists and depend on numerous factors. Also, dosing varies from one psychiatrist to the other.

The risk for adverse reactions increases with the number of medications used concurrently and with the increasing age of the patient. If you agree to take a single psychotropic or a cocktail of medicines, study the medicines and you and your prescriber ideally closely monitor symptom relief, but importantly, check for the side effects. These side effects should be discussed and documented in your medical file.

A greater reliance on nonpharmacologic treatment is a wiser choice discussed in *Healing Your Depression: A Catholic Perspective, 2ⁿᵈ Ed.* As a compromise in treatment for depression, the patient may choose to undergo regular and frequent talk therapy sessions while prescribed one or more psychotropics. The prescription provider, as a psychotropic expert, advises you and recommends.

In practice, psychiatrists rely almost entirely on diagnosing psychopathologies and writing prescriptions. They focus on the most appropriate psychotropics for your relief. They stress that a psychotropic pill or a cocktail of pills will diminish your symptoms of depression. Their focus is symptom relief. And admittedly, many patients are helped with antidepressants, sometimes twinned with antianxiety medicines.

American society favors pills for the first and immediate response to major and minor ailments. Prestigious medical journals like the *New England Journal of Medicine* and lay publications like *The New Yorker* magazine and *Consumer Reports* frequently describe America's love affair with prescription medications leading to an overmedicated America. Be reserved and become educated about overmedication in our country.

Research your prescribed psychotropics. Information is readily available from reliable medical and online governmental resources. You may wish to learn about SSRIs, SNRIs, and NMDs, as each classification influences brain chemistries differently.

You learn through experience and research that a few select antidepressants you may be prescribed are fast-acting. Some of them reach therapeutic levels for swift symptom relief within a week.

However, most psychotropics are slower-acting and often require four to six weeks to become fully effective. Patience is required. Psychiatrists sometimes fail to mention this detail. You have hopes and expectations of symptom relief, so you are wise to ask when you will feel relief.

You often learn about the side effects of your prescribed psychotropic medicine in drug commercials on television. The sad part is that often these medicines do little to ease your depression while causing discomfort.

Diagnosing, writing a prescription, and seeing a patient for a few minutes requires a very different skill set from sitting with a patient and conducting effective talk therapy for sixty minutes. The shorter visits with the prescribing psychiatrist may be limited help to you.

Anyone prescribed medicine for a mental illness should carefully study what they ingest. Become informed and do not simply trust the prescriber drugs prescribed. Study the medication insert information. Visit WebMD. Consult with the pharmacist and ask questions. Pharmacists, usually educated with a Pharm.D. degree today, are happy to educate you. Asking about medications is especially crucial if you are pregnant, breastfeeding, or taking other medicines for chronic or degenerative diseases.

Antidepressants and antianxiety medicines are limited to symptom relief and do not heal.

Faith and action first. Healing comes with prayer, church involvement, changes in your thinking, and guided self-care activities like exercise, proper nutrition intake, and enhanced relationship building.

The prescribed medications are not the solution to your depression. They may, in fact, delay healing and make the quality of your life worse if you suffer from their annoying side effects.

Taking psychotropics without effective talk therapy with a capable and effective therapist at least twice each month proves ineffective for you. Besides talking in therapy, changes in your behaviors and thinking are essential.

From your experience, you will learn that few psychiatrists conduct forty-five-minute talk therapy sessions with their patients. It is essential to ask before making an appointment if you seek talk therapy.

If you find a psychiatrist who provides effective forty-five minute or one-hour talk therapy sessions and prescribes only as needed, you have completed an excellent provider search. You are most fortunate.

If you prefer a psychiatrist only for prescription meds, expect your sessions to be brief. Psychiatric office visits usually focus on the success or failure of the prescribed drugs and are generally scheduled at twenty-minute intervals per patient.

The pharmacologic treatment orientation is derived from psychiatric residencies, which focus on DSM-5 diagnoses and PDR references to reduce the symptoms of mental illness through brain chemistry change.

You will undergo an intake or assessment visit with the psychiatrist on your first visit, which may last forty-five minutes or more. The insurance company will usually be billed at least three hundred dollars.

After that, things change for you with a diagnosis and prescriptions written. You may see the psychiatrist once every one, two, or even three months if there is symptom relief and no side effects that you find too unpleasant or unmanageable. These appointments will usually be billed at a minimum of one hundred fifty dollars.

Seeing multiple patients each hour is standard in the United States and yields robust reimbursement from the insurance companies to the agency or clinician. In contrast, symptom relief and healing for the patients are sometimes uncertain. There is an obvious need for agencies to pay clinicians' salaries with benefits and manage the overhead and fixed costs associated with building maintenance and upkeep.

However, a psychiatric patient with depression may dare to ask, "Is this really the most effective way to treat me for my mental illness?" "Will these abbreviated visits and prescriptions improve my long-term mental well-being?"

Notably, the pandemic led to social isolation and family stressors nationwide. It is no surprise that antidepressant prescription writing has increased by twenty-five percent since the beginning of the coronavirus pandemic in 2019. Pharmaceutical companies like Pfizer, Eli Lilly, and GlaxoSmithKline benefit from the millions of prescriptions written yearly for depression by psychiatrists, psychiatric nurse practitioners, and other physician extenders.

Insurance visit co-pays required of the patient can be five, fifteen, twenty-five, and even more than fifty dollars, even for short visits with the medication prescriber.

Medication check-ups without regular therapy are like paddling a rowboat with one oar; you are boating and have movement in the water, but you are going in circles.

Psychiatric Nurse Practitioners

These mental health professionals with an "MSN, NPP" credential are registered nurses with a master's (MSN) or doctoral (DPN) degree in nursing with a specialty in psychiatry. They can prescribe psychotropic medicines and are reported to conduct more extended talk therapy sessions with their patients. Their appointments with patients are usually fifty minutes in length.

Psychiatric nurse practitioners can bill health insurance companies for their services. Also, the better-quality MSN-NPP programs now provide training and practice in positive psychiatry therapy. Choosing this mental health professional, who offers more extended talk therapy, is an alternative to the psychiatrist. The costs for their services are usually more reasonable.

Mental Health Therapists

Psychologists, licensed social workers, licensed professional counselors, psychiatric nurses, and others are not legally authorized to prescribe medicines. They depend on talk therapy for their livelihood. Not all therapists are eligible to bill insurance companies for reimbursement of clinical services.

Mental health providers have attractive websites with bios that assure you they can help you. Many providers even have short videos to promote themselves and their clinical services. Before you contact any of them, study what they share on the screen. They have a variety of methods for you to reach out to them.

Experience with Therapists

You are wise to maintain the records of your mental health care. These can include your available medical records, therapists seen, and personal journal entries. If you also see a prescriber for psychotropics, keep a list of the medication's generic names and brand names with dosing, noted changes in physical and mental health, and dates.

As you engage with therapists, you learn that they tend to be empathetic, caring, and focused on lessening your anguish. They want to assist you with psychic pain relief to grow. You learn that those in the mental health profession are kind, caring, curious, and endowed with social and emotional intelligence. Most therapists will help you but, honestly, a few may not. This can be said for all health services providers.

Things to Ask About—Don't Be Shy

Are you licensed? Do you have experience conducting CBT, MET, or positive psychology? Can you see me weekly or bi-weekly? How much do you charge for each therapy session? Do you accept private insurance? Tricare? Medicare? Medicaid? Aetna? Cigna? What are the co-pays? How long is your typical therapy session? How soon can I get an appointment? Do you have any suggested reading materials or websites on depression that may help me? Do you assign homework?

These are all reasonable questions to ask your prospective candidate therapists. You are entering into an intimate, time-consuming, and expensive relationship. If they are not definitive in their answers, be cautious, as you want to avoid surprises when you begin your therapy sessions or receive your first bill from the therapist or agency.

Theoretical orientation. Ask about their preferred therapeutic modalities. For example, if you want to change your thoughts and think doing so will change your life, you might consider a cognitive therapist. Cognitive behavioral therapy (CBT) is a popular modality. Consider solution-oriented therapies if you do not want to dwell on your earlier years and only want to deal with the "here and now" issues related to your depression.

Call and talk with them. When you identify a potential therapist, call them on the phone. What is their specialty? Be cautious with therapists who offer to help with the broad spectrum of mental illnesses. Share a little about your history of depression and see how the therapist responds. Take notes of these calls.

Ask if they have the education and experience in conducting positive psychology sessions with their clients.

Mental health therapists who assert they can conduct all therapeutic modalities delude themselves. Therapeutic modalities must be studied, learned, and practiced in a clinical setting and critiqued by expert clinicians. Ask about their preferred modality. Ask about Martin Seligman's and Angela Duckworth's research and writings and the VIA Institute on Character.

Keep calling until you find someone whose style resonates with you. You may spend a lot of time on the phone with your search. Your search provides needed information, builds your confidence, and empowers you in your search efforts.

Cost for services. Based on your insurance policy or income, you may have a five, fifteen, twenty-five, or fifty-dollar co-pay for each therapy session. Build this cost into your monthly budget. Consider these dollars spent as an investment in your improved health. Maintain a file of your insurance explanations of benefits and records of your co-pays and psychotropic medicine expenses. You learn that your therapy and treatment can cost thousands of dollars over just a few months of care.

Before you set up a therapy appointment, discuss the fees. Mixing medical care with money may seem indelicate, but this discussion is essential because therapy is expensive. Wouldn't you ask for the cost of a car repair before you had the mechanic conduct the work? It is reasonable to know what your therapy costs will be.

Ask if they are eligible for reimbursement by your health insurance company. Will Medicare or Medicaid reimburse for their services rendered, or will you end up paying it all out-of-pocket? If you are on Medicare, regularly review your Explanations of Benefits (EOBs) for charges and payments for your sessions. Retain these documents.

Ask about a sliding fee scale discount if uninsured. If privately insured, what is the co-pay for each session? How many sessions are covered by your insurance? You may need to call your insurance company for details on mental health coverage, as they vary among companies.

If the therapist defers you to the business or billing office for payment answers, call or visit the office and get the details before you begin therapy. High out-of-pocket costs are a stressor, particularly during these inflationary times. If the therapist or agency is rigid in their fees, continue your search elsewhere.

If you do not have insurance and cannot afford the fees, explore seeing a psychology or counseling intern at a university counseling center. The important thing about seeing graduate student interns is that their work is often recorded and checked by a licensed and experienced therapist. The costs are always lower.

Licensure. Ethical problems and drug and alcohol impairments occur among all professionals, including mental health professionals. Have they been sued for malpractice? Were there ethical violations affecting their licensure leading to suspension?

Every state has medical and nursing boards that share public records of past complaints and ethical and legal troubles with the public. This information is free and available on the internet, and it may not necessarily disqualify them, but it provides you with additional information.

Your First Appointment

During your first appointment, did you feel heard when you spoke? Did the therapist appear to listen? Did they spend much of the time talking about themselves? Did they allow you to speak honestly and frankly about your feelings?

Sometimes it takes a couple of sessions to decide if the therapist is right for you. Do not return if you determine that the therapist is not a good match. You are taking care of yourself by choosing someone who can help you.

So again, finding a therapist who is right for you is work and takes time and energy. However, you are worth it. Remember that you can share openly and honestly with an effective therapist. It is a place for tears and hope. The focus is on you and your healing.

In therapy sessions, you have opportunities to say aloud the problematic things that repeatedly whirl through your mind and hold you back from happiness. You also have opportunities to recognize and appreciate your strengths and the beneficial and noble things you have done in your life. You eventually eliminate the painful thoughts and replace them with positive ones.

Record Keeping

Keep records of your therapist search. These can include their website addresses, notes from telephone calls, and information about the therapeutic modality and costs. These records can be reference documents in your care.

Also, keep records of your therapy sessions. Have a private notebook. Write about what you explored in your therapy sessions. What did you learn? Did the therapist provide helpful feedback or suggest specific actions for you? Was the therapist helpful? Did you leave the therapy session feeling hopeful?

Homework

Ask if your therapist does not give you activities to work on before the next session. You are a work in progress, and healing does not occur only within the confines of a therapy room for an hour each week or two. Work on recovery inside and outside of the room with assigned homework.

These homework assignments can include, for example, writing a gratitude letter to someone dear to you, calling someone to reestablish a broken relationship, improving a particular family relationship, or becoming more involved in your Catholic Church activities.

Why homework? A simile may help. Therapy is educational and a bit like taking a college course. If you take, for example, a philosophy course for three credit hours/week and attend all classes but do not read or study the subject-specific content or do homework outside of class, you learn little about philosophy. Read and work outside the therapy sessions to boost your self-knowledge and accelerate your healing.

At a minimum, complete this book's positive psychology activities at the end of each chapter for enhanced learning and healing. Discuss the completed chapter activities in therapy.

Look upon your hours inside and outside of therapy as learning experiences. Doing guided homework and reading on the subject outside the therapy room will lead to an increased understanding of mental health and more accelerated healing.

Chapter Activity: Listing the issues for discussion with the therapist

Date: _____

Spend quiet time and define the issues you wish to discuss with the therapist. What is bothering you? Briefly describe how these issues have affected you. How can the therapist assist you with these problems? Be specific.

Specific Issues for Discussion:

1. _____

2. _____

3. _____

4. _____

Notes:

List Your VIA Signature Character Strengths. How may they assist you with these issues?

1. _____

2. _____

3. _____

4. _____

5. _____

Notes:

Chapter 5
Popular Therapeutic Modalities

Have patience with all things, but chiefly have patience with yourself. Do not lose courage in considering your imperfections but instantly set about remedying them—every day, begin anew.

Saint Francis de Sales

Approaches to Solving Problems

Be patient with yourself and your participation in therapy; recognize that healing is a slow process. It requires courage to initiate a therapeutic relationship and consider which modality might be best for you. At a minimum, it is helpful to understand the fundamentals of therapy and the common modalities.

A variety of therapeutic modalities exist to guide you to mental health. It is wise to become conversant with the basics of therapy and a few mainstream therapeutic modalities. Ideally, you enter a therapist's office with basic information about the therapy field as it provides insights on what to expect and how to effectively participate in this healing milieu.

Therapy is interactive, with constructive and guided exchanges between the clinician and client. It is wise to become familiar with different modalities as it makes you a more informed consumer of therapeutic services. Therapeutic modalities follow a set of guidelines and approaches based on research, and you are wise to ask for the modality that you think may best help you heal from depression.

You may have overwhelming chronic depression, traumatic memories, anxiety attacks, and low self-esteem. You may be diagnosed with clinical depression, bipolar disorder, PTSD, and other mental health diagnoses in your intake. These are usually accurate diagnoses based on the clinician's interpretation of the tome published by the American Psychiatric Association, the *Diagnostic and Statistical Manual-5,* or the *DSM-5.* This thick volume uses a lens of psychopathology but is an essential guide for making a diagnosis or diagnoses by mental health professionals.

In years past, psychiatrists and psychiatric nurse practitioners often had a *Physician Desk Reference* (PDR) on their desks to look up medicines and their descriptions, dosages, administration, contraindications, and precautions.

But, with technological advances, the tome was migrated to the internet in 2017 as the *Prescriber's Digital Registry.* Psychiatrists, psychiatric nurse practitioners, and other physician extenders often refer to the *PDR* when preparing prescription cocktails.

Weekly or biweekly therapy sessions are essential to healing and improved mental health and well-being.

Therapy sessions every four, five, or six weeks apart waste your time. These widely spaced sessions are an adroit but shallow activity designed to create a favorable impression of care. The usual argument for this scheduling is a "full client load" and a "scarcity of therapists." Do not settle. Find another more available but capable therapist and agency by developing self-advocacy skills.

Many who suffer from depression and other mental illnesses find self-advocacy a foreign concept. But it is critical to your healing. Self-advocacy involves understanding your needs, knowing the kind of support you need, and communicating those needs to others. It leads to improved self-esteem, empowerment, and importantly, tailored mental health services to meet your needs. It is part of healing.

Ideally, you should see your therapist every week or every other week. Your treatment should be intense, and your therapist should follow a therapeutic modality. It would be best if you are given homework to complete and share in the following sessions.

With this individual therapy, you aspire to share honestly with your therapist. Be open and honest. In therapy sessions, you have opportunities to say aloud the painful things that whirl through your mind repeatedly and hold you back from mental well-being and happiness. You will eventually eliminate those thoughts and replace them with positive thoughts with therapy.

Popular Modalities

According to the American Psychology Association (APA), therapists generally draw on one or more theories of psychotherapy. A "theory" in psychotherapy is a roadmap for therapists to guide them through understanding their clients and their problems and cooperatively developing solutions.

Those who have taken a high school psychology course will recall the names of famous researchers and practitioners such as B.F. Skinner, Sigmund Freud, Ivan Pavlov, Albert Ellis, William James,

Abraham Maslow, and Carl Rogers. More recent famous notables include Martin Seligman, Barbara Fredrickson, Ed Diener, Angela Duckworth, and Mihaly Csikszentmihalyi. All have contributed to the fields of human behavior, psychotherapy, and mental health.

Approaches to psychotherapy fall into five broad categories: psychoanalysis and psychodynamic therapy, behavioral therapy, desensitization, cognitive therapy, humanistic therapy, and holistic or integrative therapy. It is important to note that many therapists only adhere to one approach, although some report blending elements from different approaches and tailoring their therapeutic techniques according to each client's needs.

There are dozens of therapeutic modalities today by a variety of names.

However, five forms of therapy are reported on and tend to be more frequently used. These include:

- Cognitive Behavioral Therapy (CBT)

- Motivational Enhancement Therapy (MET)

- Couples and Family Therapy

- Holistic Therapy

- Positive Psychology Therapy

All therapies have commonalities. The therapist focuses on relating to the client, paying attention to what they have to say, recognizing their cognitive biases and how they think, and suggesting and teaching. The therapist and client pursue solutions and seek healing and well-being.

For a comprehensive explanation of the modalities, browser search "NIMH and psychotherapies" and "commonly used psychotherapies." The "Very Well Mind" website, with content reviewed by psychiatrists, is also informative.

Cognitive Behavioral Therapy

CBT is a popular therapeutic modality used to improve mental health. CBT can be short or long-term. It takes a hands-on, practical approach to problem-solving, and its goal is to change your patterns of thinking and behavior and change how you feel. CBT is a valuable tool to change your thinking and behavioral coping mechanisms. It is meant to improve your mood and enhance your coping strategies.

CBT is different from traditional talk therapies. It is skill-based and focuses on the present day, although you consider your past. It requires your active participation in the treatment. For example, your therapist may give you written assignments outside the office that can improve your mood through positive self-reflection. They may ask you to read a select book or visit helpful websites which you discuss in therapy.

Collaborate with the therapist and cooperatively set definitive goals for your therapy. These can be simple declarative statements. Prioritize the issues you wish to work on. These goals should be written down and reviewed periodically.

CBT can be a healing modality and assist you with identifying unhealthy thought patterns and seeking solutions.

CBT can raise you from survival mode and assist you in making better choices in your life. It helps track dysfunctional thoughts. Some suggest that CBT guides you in re-establishing healthy thinking patterns.

CBT teaches you to recognize your moods, thoughts, and situations that trigger harmful or high-risk behaviors. Then, the therapist may assist you in replacing negative thoughts and feelings with healthy ones. The healthy feelings and ideas resulting from CBT improve your mood and self-concept. In addition, the skills you learn with CBT can last you a lifetime.

Also, CBT helps with problem-solving by revealing aloud your beliefs, thoughts, and feelings. Through CBT, you learn that perceptions directly influence your responses to specific situations. Thought processes inform and lead you to change behaviors and actions and improve your mood.

CBT is grounded in the belief that people's perception will determine their actions. It is not the events themselves that determine your actions or feelings but your perceptions.

For example, a person diagnosed with "major clinical depression" in accordance with the DSM-5 criteria, may look through a lens of misfortune. They may believe everything will turn out badly on a given day. These negative thoughts influence their focus for the day. They may only perceive negative things that happen throughout the day and not register or recognize the good things.

During the day, they may block out or avoid thoughts or actions that disprove their opposing beliefs. Perhaps some happy things happen, but they ignore them. Afterward, when nothing appears to go right in the day, they feel even more depressed than before. Through a continued negative belief system, the depression heightens, and they can be confined to a continuous cycle of depression. They end up having a series of lousy days, weeks, and months.

You are strolling in a park in rural New Hampshire on a winter's day, and it begins to rain. Rather than complain about the rain, you might instead be thankful for the needed rainfall and grateful that the precipitation is not sleet or a wet snow. Perceptions count.

Jayme Albin and Eileen Bailey have authored an excellent book on CBT. *Cognitive Behavioral Therapy: Recognize and Overcome Behaviors for a Healthier, Happier Us* was published by DK Penguin Random House in 2021. Aside from examining depression, it discusses anxiety, eating disorders, grief, positive body image, controlling anger, and relationship enhancement.

The topic of happiness is also included and discussed in the closing chapter of *Healing Your Depression: A Catholic Perspective, 2ⁿᵈ Ed.* Pope Francis, among others, shares his wisdom on happiness and faith.

In conclusion, and according to substantial current research, CBT is an effective therapeutic modality worth exploring. A word of caution is offered. If you request it, CBT guidelines should be known and followed by the therapist. Note that if the therapist does not actively engage with you in CBT and prefers to be a nodding listener or guides all your sessions into rehashing painful traumas, you may wish to speak up about the direction of the therapy and request redirection to CBT. In some cases, a therapist change might be required for your healing.

Motivational Enhancement Therapy

Motivational enhancement therapy (MET) focuses on increasing a person's motivation to change. This therapeutic approach helps you resolve your uncertainty or ambivalence about mental health therapy.

MET can be short or long-term and is intended to evoke rapid and internally motivated change.

This modality usually consists of an initial assessment session and two or more therapy sessions. An assessment is conducted in the first session. In the second therapy session, the therapist provides feedback from the initial evaluation, which stimulates discussion about personal behaviors and encourages self-motivational statements by the client.

The therapist is empathetic in these sessions and encourages you to identify specific changes in your behavior. The therapeutic relationship is a partnership. Coping strategies for high-risk situations are suggested and discussed in these sessions. In subsequent sessions, the therapist monitors changes, reviews the thinking strategies, and encourages a commitment to change.

You can bring a spouse, partner, or significant other to the MET sessions because MET can be uplifting and life-changing for you and your significant other. It is a powerful therapy for change and does not require months of weekly or biweekly therapy sessions.

MET can reduce substance abuse to alcohol, prescription drugs, or illegal substances. Researchers report that MET is used successfully with marijuana-dependent adults when combined with CBT. Thus, the combination constitutes a more comprehensive therapeutic approach.

MET focuses on increasing motivation by raising awareness of a problem, adjusting self-defeating thoughts regarding the problem, and growing confidence in your ability to change. It tackles your long-held excuses for inaction. Instead of identifying a problem and telling you what to do about it, the therapist encourages you to make self-motivating statements that display your understanding of the problem and your decision to change. Ideally, you initiate formative behavioral change.

MET can be used as a standalone therapy. However, it is usually employed in conjunction with other forms of treatment, including CBT. This combination reinforces the motivation to change. MET is different from some of the traditional therapies that often focus only on your psychopathologies.

In their writings, Martin Seligman, Ph.D. and Tayyab Rashid, Ph.D. discuss the concept of post-traumatic growth. It is worth your time to browser search MET and post-traumatic growth to learn more about these topics. Seligman and Rashid encourage therapists to employ MET with post-traumatic growth therapy for those who suffer from traumas. It can lead to a future without psychic pain and relieve depression.

Empathy and curiosity by the therapist towards the client are facets of therapy. For example, the therapist might ask, "What do you think you can do about this problem?" In asking this, they are encouraging you to use your problem-solving skills. Whatever response is expressed, the therapist can help you navigate and consider what is helpful as you make formative decisions for change.

MET is helpful in "rewiring" or changing your thinking. It allows you to think about healthy solutions with the therapist as the guide and helper. It leads you to start trusting your thinking and decision-making. You are the activist and the therapist, your advisor.

MET motivates you to recognize and build your strengths; it requires you to be gutsy in making changes. You begin by making small choices with the therapist's help and then move towards more challenging decisions.

Couples and Family Therapy

People who suffer from depression often have relationship problems with their spouse or partner, siblings, children, and friends. Focus and try not to allow your depression to harm your relationships with the people you love.

Instead, you can save and even strengthen your marriage and family relationships with therapy. If you are in an intact marital relationship, therapy can be a lifesaver for you, your spouse or partner, and your family members. These connections can be transformed through couples and family therapy.

This therapy is based on the concept that our relationships can improve if we work on them. Remember that depression affects your life and the lives of your entire family. Even extended family members like cousins, aunts, uncles, and grandparents can be affected by your depression and can be helped. Your core and extended family members can be invited into family therapy.

Couples and family therapy recognizes that the family can be a positive and powerful force for change and healing in a person's life.

This therapy modality makes the depressed person more likely to remain in treatment and succeed in getting well. The ongoing therapy is a gift in seeing family members heal and grow in the therapeutic process.

At the same time, family members can begin to recover from the disappointments and hurt caused in their lives by your depression. More honest and sincere relationships develop with work in this therapy.

Couples and family therapy can be a place for forgiveness. Emotional wounds and disappointments can leave family members with lasting feelings of anger, bitterness, and even vengeance. By embracing forgiveness, you, your partner, and your family members can embrace peace and hope through open and honest dialogue. Forgiveness leads you to emotional and spiritual well-being. Opening and closing these sessions with prayers familiar to the family can add calm to the discussions.

The couples and family therapy modality lowers divorce rates and increases family happiness among couples and family members. Parents who are clinically depressed often have difficulties in parenting their children, and these difficulties can be discussed openly.

In addition, this therapy modality helps children better manage their feelings and their lives inside and outside their homes. This treatment can be conducted on the weekends or in the evenings allowing more extensive attendance by family members.

Recovering Couples Anonymous (RCA) is a reliable and trustworthy option if you are in a troubled couple or marital relationship. RCA is a twelve-step program open to all couples wanting to build a better relationship. It has both in-person and online meetings. Couples should not delay until the relationship fails to join the RCA program.

The program has free mutual-help meetings and is easily joined on the internet and in person in local communities. Their website is readily available with a simple internet search. Their literature is helpful, and the mutual support from the meetings is reported to save and even strengthen marriages.

You and your partner may visit the RCA website, study the literature, and contact a group member for information about meetings and attendance. Read the literature, follow their 12-step program, and participate. These actions can strengthen a damaged relationship. Participation can lead to increased intimacy, enhanced communication, and a renewed commitment to remain in the relationship. This free program saves countless marriages.

Holistic Therapy

Holistic therapy theory advocates that a person's consciousness is not housed in any part of the person's body but integrates the mind, the body, and the spirit. Holistic therapy is a form of therapy that focuses on recovering through several activities. It approaches the complex nature of depression and uses a variety of approaches.

Holistic therapy is often used to manage both depression and anxiety. It can stabilize your sad moods and relieve physical ailments. Traumas leading to PTSD and other forms of abuse earlier in life are treated with holistic therapy. This therapy is more complicated than the other therapies discussed and is more than sitting with a therapist in the office weekly or biweekly.

Holistic therapy includes several activities conducted by the client simultaneously inside and outside the therapist's office.

The client may engage in positive psychology, CBT, or MET in the therapist's office. But additional activities are added, for example, practicing hatha yoga, transcendental meditation, and mindfulness. Clients in holistic therapy may also be encouraged to meet with a registered dietician (RD) for dietary advice, exercise at the gym with a personal trainer, and enjoy a periodic therapeutic massage.

The U.S. National Center for Complementary and Integrative Health (NCCIH) reports that these holistic therapy practices are now recognized by mainstream medicine. You may choose to collaborate with a physician. It is not unusual today to find board-certified physicians who practice integrative medicine in the community and subscribe to these activities for their patients.

The activities can enhance spiritual, emotional, and physical health and guide you towards healthier and clearer thinking. For example, yoga and meditation promote physical and emotional awareness. These qualities can help you recognize distressing feelings and respond better rather than only reacting to them. Massage, breathing work, and positive affirmation recitations can bring calm and comfort to a stress-filled body and an overactive and anxious mind.

Daily morning and evening meditation can have long-term positive effects on your outlook on life. Meditation can increase your patience and perseverance in therapy for depression.

Holistic therapy benefits those who are depressed and rely heavily on alcohol or illicit recreational drugs to cope. By better managing their stressors and calming their minds and bodies, meditation reduces and even eliminates cravings for alcohol and drugs. A person's mind becomes sharper without harmful substances.

Acupressure or acupuncture can stimulate naturally occurring hormones in the body that promote calmness and well-being. Enjoying a massage, participating in yoga and meditation classes, and engaging in art and music therapy will sometimes be included in holistic therapy. These activities outside the therapist's office can be both time-consuming and costly to conduct but can be worth it.

Investigate holistic therapy activities available in your community while under the care of an integrative medicine physician and psychotherapist. Keep them abreast of your ancillary activities in the community.

Positive Psychology

Positive psychology is the scientific study of the innate virtues and strengths that enable persons to thrive. It was established as a field of study at the University of Pennsylvania in Philadelphia in the 1990s. The university has a Positive Psychology Center that promotes research, education, and dissemination of positive psychology information. Visit the Positive Psychology Center website for educational materials, conferences, surveys, podcasts, books, and research reports.

Before the development of the positive psychology field, most mental health treatments were focused on the diagnosed illnesses of individuals. Traditional mental health treatment continues to label the client with, for example, a mood disorder, an anxiety disorder, OCD, a trauma and stress-related disorder, or a psychotic disorder. This labeling, which uses ICD-10 codes and DSM-5 diagnostic criteria, is mainly for health insurance reimbursement to the therapist or agency caring for the client.

While labeling and coding are essential, there is a critical paradigm shift with the use of this therapy. Positive Psychology considers what makes a person healthy and happy by identifying and then focusing on, celebrating, and employing character strengths that they possess regardless of their mental illness—including depression.

The lenses used with positive psychology are self-affirmation and hope.

Rather than look at what is wrong with you, positive psychology focuses on what is strong with you.

Positive psychology is the study of what makes life most worth living. It is the research of positive living and flourishing on various levels, including the biological, personal, relational, institutional, cultural, spiritual, and global dimensions of life. Its application improves the quality of a client's life.

Positive psychology involves "the good life" everyone can experience regardless of their situation. It considers the most significant values in a person's life– those factors that contribute most to a well-lived and fulfilling life.

The field of positive psychology was a reaction to psychoanalysis and behaviorism, which focused on mental illness and its emphasis and focus on cataloging and describing maladaptive behaviors and negative thinking. Visit your local community library or bookstore and spend a few minutes reading the Diagnostic and Statistical Manual (DSM-5) to understand this cataloging and sickness orientation better.

The first DSM volume was published in 1952 by the American Psychiatric Association with a long and detailed psychopathology list. The DSM, with later editions, continues to be the critical reference tool employed by most mental health professionals and health insurance companies to justify insurance reimbursement. It provides information from a traditional sickness viewpoint and is an essential reference publication for mental health professionals.

In formally developing the field of positive psychology, Martin Seligman, Ph.D., and his colleagues conducted rigorous research. They determined through extensive research-based studies with hundreds of thousands of people that three qualities are associated with well-being and happiness.

Well-being and happiness can be defined, measured, and enhanced.

This is a profound change in therapeutic orientation, and with this alternative orientation, one can see through the lenses of hope and encouragement with anticipation of healing and improved well-being.

The positive psychology approach, however, was not a new treatment construct formulated by Seligman in 2004. His predecessors who emphasized positive psychology concepts included William James (1892-1987), identified as the father of positive psychology, Carl Rogers (1902-1987), Abraham Maslow (1908-1970), and Edward Diener (1946-2021).

These earlier psychiatrists and psychologists were pioneers and innovators as they looked at their client's strengths rather than focusing only on their psychopathologies. They would discuss happiness, positive self-concepts, hope, and growth in their writings and therapies. Their lenses in collaborating with clients were problem-solving, healing, and hope.

The positive psychology field is based on solid, experiential research in the United States and other advanced countries, including Australia, the United Kingdom, France, Germany, and Italy. Fortune 500 companies are now embracing the tenants of positive psychology. They are doing so with continuing education to improve employee satisfaction, enhance company communications, and increase employee performance.

Positive psychology is now a part of the school curriculum and taught and practiced in elementary, middle, and high schools in France, Italy, and the Netherlands. European students are learning about the positive psychology paradigm and their personal character strengths in combating depression, anxiety, loneliness, and bullying.

The school curriculum content is affirming, preventive, and healing, leading to improvements in the students' lives and the quality of education. Positive psychology encourages an emphasis on happiness, well-being, and positivity.

In therapy, positive psychologists suggest ways that individual happiness may be fostered in the client. For example, you can recognize, appreciate, and apply your character strengths daily rather than dwell on your weaknesses.

This therapy can strengthen social ties with a spouse or partner, family members, friends, and the more extensive networks with employment, faith-based groups, civic clubs, and social organizations. Physical exercise, meditation, and mindfulness are encouraged while in therapy and after, which can contribute to happiness and recovery from depression and anxiety.

Positive psychology can add without replacing or ignoring traditional talk therapies while improving self-esteem and self-image.

This therapy helps balance the other therapeutic approaches focusing on DSM-5 mental health disorders. Positive psychology techniques encourage clients to think differently and more positively about themselves and those around them.

The premise of positive psychology is that you should consider the past but draw from and focus on the present. This change in orientation affects how you think about the nature of your happiness. Therefore, clients in positive psychology therapy are encouraged to work on personal growth regardless of how pronounced or debilitating the depression may seem.

Positive Psychology fosters a cheerful outlook toward your past life experiences. This optimistic view is essential to you in therapy. The goal is to minimize negative thoughts that may arise with a hopeless mindset and instead develop a sense of hope and optimism about your future.

Therapists who employ positive psychology in their practices encourage their clients to accept the past and develop positive anticipation of the future. These thoughts lead to a sense of well-being in the present and help recognize their strengths. It brings them hope for the future.

In addition, positive psychology helps you to love yourself and others more profoundly and encourages you to recognize and reinforce your goodness instead of thinking about the negative things in your life.

When you embrace positive psychology as your chosen therapeutic modality, you look at and enhance the good within yourself with the therapist as your guide.

The field of positive psychology thrives in master's and doctoral education programs in psychology and counseling in the United States. Fellowships and residencies in integrative psychiatry are becoming mainstream in medicine. Multiple graduate programs in the United States offer students opportunities to earn a Ph.D. in Positive Psychology. It has become a recognized and popular therapeutic modality. Whether a client chooses to undergo as few as six bi-weekly therapy sessions or many months of ongoing therapy, it works because it is effective.

Also, it is being taught to college and university students at the undergraduate and graduate levels. Three-credit hour positive psychology courses are reported to be extremely popular at, for example, the University of Pennsylvania, Yale, Harvard, and the University of North Carolina at Chapel Hill.

These positive psychology classes are filled with thousands of students each year, leading to happier students, fewer university medical clinic visits for physical ailments, and fewer mental health crisis visits to their university counseling centers. These positive psychology courses are buffers against homesickness, stress, depression, anxiety, and other ailments affecting students in the college and university setting.

Mental health clinicians reading this book may are asked to visit Google Scholar and PubMed for multiple valid research reports on the more severely mentally ill with borderline personality disorder and schizophrenia. Learn about how effective Positive Psychology interventions are a complement to their treatment. The interventions were reported to greatly reduce symptomatology and improve the quality of life among those struggling with these illnesses. Well-being was reported to improve across those in the multiple randomized controlled trials (RCT) and meta-analyses.

PERMA Model

Martin Seligman, Ph.D., at the University of Pennsylvania, developed a summary of the components of positive psychology that combine to create the PERMA Model. Many therapists use this model in practice. Also, those who seek to help themselves with depression relief outside of therapy adhere to the model.

One of the cornerstones of positive psychology is the PERMA Model. You focus on the good in your past and consider the present. The PERMA Model is found throughout the literature in psychology and on the internet. A simple browser search of the PERMA Model presents dozens of explanations and applications for its use.

The Positive Psychology website is informative and includes explanations, videos, strengths discussions, graphics, and exercises. It is worth memorizing and posting the model with its five elements on your refrigerator door as a daily reminder.

Daily use of the PERMA Model can help to reduce depression and lead to improved well-being.

Daily considerations of the PERMA elements by those who are depressed lead to mood boosts. The five elements of the model are as follows:

P – Positive Feelings. Your feelings are a choice. This element has one of the most obvious connections to happiness. When you experience positive feelings, you experience joy, contentment, hope, gratitude, optimism, trust, confidence, and pride. These positive feelings can be about your past, present, and future. You can take the time to savor these feelings.

Positive feelings involve being optimistic and positively viewing the past, present, and future. It is easy and even automatic to ruminate over failures and traumas. However, a positive view of your life can help improve the picture of yourself and your relationships. A more optimistic view can inspire you to be more hopeful and lead to making positive life changes.

Focusing on the lows in life increases your depression. However, like learning any new skill, you can increase the joys and positive aspects of life by consciously choosing to focus on positive feelings. You can, in a sense, "rewire" your brain to foster positive thoughts instead of negative thoughts. What you think about is a choice.

There are also many emotional and physical health benefits to optimism and positivity. Not only does your mental health improve, but recent research suggests that putting efforts into positivity increases your resistance to the common cold and improves your physical health, emotional coping skills, and sleep quality.

Your immune system is strengthened. It is reported that your positive emotions make you more resistant to the corona, RSV, and flu viruses.

Developing more positive feelings helps you to enjoy life more. You become more resilient and face challenges by choosing creative and alternative solutions to them. You can build spiritual and emotional armor to manage your depression more effectively, and the PERMA Model helps you do this.

Take a moment and think about your last two days. Did you encounter any stressful situations? How did you manage them? Could you have better engaged your positive feelings in your actions? Could you have responded to a problem more effectively?

You can discuss these issues with your priest, therapist, and those close to you. Be brave and discuss your feelings about life events. Do not be afraid to cry about them in therapy or with your immediate family members and friends.

E – Engagement. Finding activities that need full engagement is vital to increasing your well-being and nurturing your happiness. Everyone is different, and everyone finds engagement in different things.

Engagement can be absorption in, for example, gardening, walking foot trails, journaling, creative writing, listening to your favorite music, participating in sports activities, creating art or music, reading your favorite literature genres, or engaging in spiritual and faith-based community activities. As mentioned in an earlier chapter, your Catholic Church can become your second home and a place of spiritual engagement, solace, and calm.

Besides physical exercise, engage in spiritual activities daily. This spiritual engagement can involve reciting your Catholic prayers, reading Catholic literature, frequently attending Mass, and listening to church music daily. Through this spiritual engagement, you experience serenity and peace. You are reminded that Jesus listens to your prayers and is always by your side.

Remember that the Holy Spirit can inspire and guide you with His gifts, including knowledge of right from wrong, courage in demanding situations, and piety. The Holy Spirit showers you with grace to act with self-control, modesty, chastity, and faithfulness.

Mix your activities up with a varied schedule to make them stimulating. In addition, join in positive social interactions with like-minded people. Consider an ecumenical Bible study, a book club, a volunteer agency, or a civic organization. Perhaps volunteer at your Catholic Church food pantry or Habitat for Humanity. These engaging activities are antidotes to depression and enhance your well-being as you seek to participate with and help others. You meet friendly people in the process.

Each of us needs one or more things in life that absorb us into the present and mindful moment. Ideally, you have one or two activities that create a bliss-filled immersion in the tasks. Engagement is essential in stretching your intelligence, skills, and emotional capabilities. Positive attention is crucial, and when you are engaged in these activities that you immensely enjoy, it enhances your overall well-being.

R – *Relationships*. Researchers consistently report that happy people have warm and supportive relationships. Your social health deals with these connections with others. It involves kindness to and from others, friendships, and deep, authentic relationships with trust. Mental health professionals assert that developing more positive relationships with family, friends, and co-workers enhances your well-being and buffers you from depression.

Do not allow the coronavirus aftermath to prevent you from spending quality time with your friends. Mask up if necessary and meet in person at the local Starbucks or Barnes & Noble cafés. Alternatively, Zoom or call them each week. Commit to maintaining and even enhancing your friendships in 2023 and beyond.

Positive and supportive relationships are crucial to your mental health. These relationships can be the most critical aspects of your life as they enhance your sense of belonging. We are social animals and should not be alone or isolate ourselves. We thrive on connections, love, intimacy, and healthy emotional and physical interaction with others.

You can enhance positive relationships with a spouse or partner, children, parents, siblings, peers, and friends to spread love and joy. The PERMA Model encourages you to examine relationships and connections and repair or improve them through thoughtful communications and actions.

It is essential to develop positive and healthy relationships to support you. Realize that it may mean disengaging from those acquaintances who are judgmental and angry with life; they bring you down. Strengthen your current friendships and make new friends.

Those who experience severe clinical depression sometimes progress to the point where their primary focus in life is on themselves and their burdensome mental and physical illnesses. As their depression worsens, their behaviors narrow, their thinking becomes obsessive, and they spend their time and effort being anxious over their conditions.

They may stay in bed nearly all day, make poor food choices, and constantly play videogames, or max out on Netflix or Freevee TV. They rarely leave their bedroom and, sadly, are resistant to the help offered by a spouse or parent. It is time to get unstuck.

This sickness orientation needs to change to a more positive one. Helping and compassionate relationships can support severely depressed people to guide them to healing actions. This can be through kind words of encouragement, and pleasant church, home, and community activities.

Solid relationships can support you during your challenging times, whether it is a death in the family, a monetary crisis, or a disappointment at work. The quality of your relationships is more important than the actual number. Consider and be grateful for those you can call on when you are depressed. You can think about the quality of the relationships and how they improve the quality of your life. The number of relationships is secondary.

For some of us, the number of close friends who care about us and raise us up when we struggle with depression can often be counted on one hand. God brings these good people into our lives in His compassion for us.

Suicide ideation is common with severe depression. Some suffer from suicide ideation and concoct a definitive plan for dying. Or they may become so distressed that they consider hurting others. They should not simmer with these thoughts or hesitate to seek help. This is a time to reach out to another for help.

Those contemplating suicide should go or be transported by a family member or close friend to a medical center with a psychiatric unit. They can enter through the emergency department (ED) and state that they wish to be voluntarily hospitalized in the psychiatric unit because they are "suicidal and harmful to themselves or others."

With the overriding concern for responsive medical care delivery and the avoidance of possible family litigation resulting from a completed suicide, hospitalization is highly likely regardless of health insurance status.

The nurses in ED intake will understand and comply, and the patient will be promptly assessed by a physician and registered for admission. The suicidal person may be in the unit within hours. With this brave action, the person suffering from severe depression may have saved their life or the life of another.

The federal government's Agency for Healthcare Research and Quality reports that between 2008 and 2017, the number of ED visits only for suicide ideation and suicide attempts increased. In 2017 alone, there were over one million registered suicide-related ED visits.

With the pandemic onset and between the fall of 2019 and fall 2020, hospitalizations for suicide ideation and attempts increased by fifty-seven percent. This is a severe public health problem that few academics or public health professionals are discussing.

Healthy relationships are formed through active participation in social groups. These can be organizations like faith-based communities and civic organizations like the Lions Club and Rotary. In addition, you can find new connections in religious or recreational organizations. Befriend those who are on a similar transformative path of growth in life. We can consciously surround ourselves with positive people.

Rely heavily on your Catholic Church community and attend weekday noon Masses if possible. Join a gym or wellness center and visit during the week. These are great ways to spend time throughout the week.

Weekday Mass attendance will comfort you; seek out friends and spiritual companions through church activities. Work out daily at the gym by lap swimming, aqua yoga, occasional brisk walks on the indoor track, or Pilates classes. The relationships and the camaraderie developed with your church and work-out colleagues can become meaningful.

M – Meaning. The concept of meaning involves purpose with having goals and a direction in your life. Meaning consists of the degree to which you believe your life has value, worth, and importance. Purpose-filled routines usually characterize your life. Meaning makes you feel your life has significance beyond the trivial or momentary. Life can have a purpose that transcends boredom.

Meaning cannot be pursued as a goal. Instead, it arises from pursuing other goals. Ideally, you let it happen by not caring about it and, instead, embrace activities that connect you with something greater than yourself. This may be the pursuit of parenting to the best of your ability, dedicating yourself to the care of your elderly parents, committing yourself to the care of others through volunteer work, earning a college degree, taking a writing class, or finally getting fit.

Having meaning in your life is not something that comes by chance. Meaning comes when you use your talents and strengths to serve something you view as consequential. Having a purpose is vital to living a life of happiness and fulfillment. It is not the pursuit of only pleasure or material wealth.

The minimalists in our society would suggest that the essential things in life that give us meaning are not things. Meaning gives us a reason and purpose for our lives regardless of age, occupation, social status, or possessions.

If your depression seems devastating, Emotions Anonymous (EA) may become helpful to you. EA was established in 1971 and is a fellowship of people wanting to improve their emotional well-being; the only requirement for membership is the desire to increase emotional well-being. Membership in EA can bring meaning into your life. You can appreciate the emotional support as a member and realize that you are not alone in your depression.

EA is a global 12-step recovery program that focuses on emotional health improvement. It is free and readily available with in-person and online meetings. The EA 12-step program has vital and beneficial spiritual elements involving "a god of our understanding" and "a power greater than ourselves" for guidance, recovery, and healing. The reading materials available on their website are instructive. EA can be reached by searching the internet, and their international office is in Saint Paul at 651-647-9712.

A – Accomplishments. You have accomplished things in life and benefit from naming and recognizing them. A worthwhile task is to list them on a piece of paper. Your accomplishments include raising a family, helping others, earning employment successes, sports performance, college degrees, and completing significant life tasks. These are things you can be proud of and savor.

Feelings of success and pride come from meeting your personal and professional goals. Positive feelings come not only after the goal is met, but also while it is pursued. Too often, we set up situations where we say, "I will be happy if I finish my college degree, complete a work project, or purchase a home or new automobile." But happiness is experienced in accomplishing goals.

Americans love cliches, and we often say, "the journey of a thousand miles begins with the first step." Gradual movement forward will give you a sense of satisfaction as you progress towards goal completion and finally reach that goal.

You can accomplish a goal by doing the activities suggested at the end of each chapter of *Healing Your Depression: A Catholic Perspective, 2nd Ed.* Other goals may include reading the recommended resilience and positive psychology books, visiting the websites mentioned, and becoming more involved in your local Catholic Church.

Learn to enjoy the journey out of your depression and into mental wellness. Having accomplishments in life leads you to thrive and flourish. An excellent example of achievement is getting emotionally and physically healthy through your cumulative focused actions, routines, and thought processes over time.

Application of the PERMA Model

While you work with the PERMA Model and its five elements, you can encourage your family members to read about PERMA and apply it to their lives. The model benefits everyone, and everyone can benefit from it—even if they are in peak mental and physical health. Healing can occur among your family members as you reduce and even end your depression. The model and its elements can become the subject of uplifting family dinnertime conversations.

Be attentive to the PERMA Model and its application in your daily life. Memorize and refer to the five elements of the model daily. You can apply the elements to each aspect of your daily journey in healing. Think positively about the model at home, work, and in social settings.

Learn to name what makes you happy, feel fully engaged with others, and conduct activities that bring you contentment. You can set goals towards achieving more and challenging yourself further in the activities you enjoy. Focus on the relationships with your family and friends by finding ways to connect better and enjoy each other's company more.

Mental Exercises

Let us become fully aware of our strengths and how they can help us enhance our well-being. The more strengths we use, the more well-being we have. Exercises based on research conducted by positive psychologists are presented. These exercises are not just warmhearted fuzzy feel-good ideas but tested and proven activities to lift your mood.

These exercises are not only to be kind to others but also to ourselves. If you want physical health, you must exercise regularly. It would be terrific to be in great shape without exercising and admire our home gym equipment taking up space in our bedrooms or stored in a closet or the garage. Sadly, it does not work that way.

Aside from physical exercise, there are activities that lead to happiness and well-being. You can begin these activities now. Remember that the more you practice a specific activity, the better you become at that activity.

Extend yourself to others. Smile more often. Say hello to strangers. Introduce yourself to someone at the gym or church after a workout or a Mass. Bravely extend yourself in church and learn the names of those in the pews next to you with whom you offer the "sign of peace" at each Mass. Recognize that we are brothers and sisters in Christ. We are family.

Cultivate optimism and expect a bright future. Learn to look at the bright side of things. Give yourself the benefit of the doubt. Feel good about your future. Ideally, you are feeling progress and getting better through the efforts discussed in *Healing Your Depression: A Catholic Perspective, 2nd Ed.* You are learning new routines for living life well.

Ponder your best possible self. Who would you like to become today, tomorrow, and in the future? What new goals are you considering? Besides your therapist, share these thoughts with your friends. Be open and transparent. If they are indeed your friends, they will support you with a "Great idea! Go for it. Let me know how I can help." Review the *Better Version of Myself* activity at the end of Chapter 2 and consider any changes from your first effort. Have you made any lasting changes that are now a part of your routines? Are you seeing personal growth?

You enter therapy with strengths and virtues for you to think about. Write about the character strengths you learned through your time with the VIA Character Institute website. Share these character strengths with close friends. Feel good about your strengths.

Avoid comparisons. Remember, "Thou shalt not covet thy neighbor's wife and thou shalt not covet thy neighbor's goods." You can become unhappy when you compare yourself with others. The issues you covet can involve their physical appearance, disposable income, homes, vehicles, stock portfolio, physical health, or career successes. They may have excelled where you have not. Call it luck. Maybe they just got lucky because they made shrewd decisions and worked hard and smart through the years.

You cannot envy others and be happy at the same time.

Comparing yourself with others leads you to self-disapproval as you worry about what others own or achieve. You are wiser to use your own internal standards to judge yourself rather than others' performance or appearance. It is healthier to delight in others' good fortune. Share in their joy.

Be happy for others and their triumphs. Moreover, tell them you are glad for them. Tell them they have been blessed with their good fortune resulting from wise decisions.

Look at the personal successes in your life rather than compare. Revise your thinking to focus on your growth and achievements through the years. Use a joyful lens as you look at your successes.

Spend time being grateful. Remind yourself of how grateful you can be. These can be great or unimportant things in your life. Focus on what is good in your life rather than what you think you lack.

It is not happiness that brings you gratitude, but gratitude that brings you happiness.

This concept is worth repeating. It is not happiness that brings you gratitude, but gratitude that brings you happiness. Pause and take a few moments to think about the abundance of what God has blessed you with in your life. Take the time and list them on a sheet of paper. Carry the list with you in your wallet or purse as a reminder.

Peruse the dozens of recently published and helpful books on gratitude in your libraries, the Amazon bookstore, and the mental health section of your local bookstores. Read a few. Remind yourself how fortunate you are.

Visit the YouTube channel for dozens of gratitude videos. Seek out the Catholic prayers of affirmations posted on the YouTube platform. Also, as mentioned in Chapter 2, Bob Baker and Louise L. Hay have dozens of gratitude affirmation recordings you can enjoy.

Practice acts of kindness. Be kind to those around you. Use the lens of kindness, especially with those who are suffering. Ideally, do things for people not because of who they are or what they may do in return but because of who you are. As you search for ways to heal yourself from your depression, you learn that kindness to others reduces your depression. When you commit acts of service, you see yourself as charitable and compassionate. This thinking promotes confidence, optimism, and feelings of usefulness, and you sense the Holy Spirit working within you by guiding you in your efforts.

Encourage others. It gives you a sense of goodness and humanness when you nurture your relationships by encouraging others to talk about their accomplishments and successes in life. Be mindful, listen, and let them speak about things that make them happy. This is not a time for making comparisons.

Do not feel compelled to interrupt with comparisons or finish another's sentences. Happy people are good listeners and want to hear what others want to share. They are good at communicating with family members, friends, and even strangers. Encouraging others involves being available for others to talk. You listen first, and you can talk later.

Researchers report that kindness is a major feature of intelligence. In other words, good people are the smartest people. Neurobiologist Richard Davidson says that "the foundation of a healthy and thinking brain is kindness." He explains that kindness requires the ability to think not only about ourselves but also about others. There is also a high positive correlation between compassion and intellect.

Commit more quality time to your spouse or partner, children, and friends. Could you treat them with greater kindness, compassion, and be more encouraging? You can also listen to and take an interest in your colleagues at work and people in your church community and civic organizations.

As this chapter closes, you are ideally more aware of popular therapeutic modalities, including CBT, MET, couples and family therapy, holistic therapy, and positive psychology. You and your family have also learned about the PERMA Model, and you have taped the model to your refrigerator door for daily reference and reflection.

You have learned about what to expect from a therapist and a therapy session. Remember that therapy is not meandering talk time. It is not hashing, rehashing, and further rehashing the sad times leading to self-deprecation and more profound depression. It involves focused discussion and action by you and the therapist as you work on healing and improving your mental health.

With God's grace, you are empowered and doing the healing in cooperation with a skilled therapist.

Be concerned if you request a particular modality, like positive psychology or CBT, and the clinician does not follow through. Perhaps the therapist needs to study the modality and be more skilled with its use. Therapists commonly use those methods they learned and practiced in graduate school or their medical residencies; they use those with which they are most comfortable. If you are making progress in healing with the therapist's style, stay with it. However, requesting another therapist versed in a particular modality is reasonable. In therapy, you learn what works best for you with the therapy and therapist.

Therapy is focused work for the therapist and the client. You want to leave the session more enlightened and hopeful. Ideally, you feel better about yourself, family, and the world. Crying repeatedly over past mistakes using "should have" and "could have" statements is counterproductive in therapy sessions. Therapists versed in positive psychology are aware of this.

Also, if you complete three or four sessions and do not feel as though you are feeling better and receiving the guidance you need to heal, first discuss this matter with the therapist. Without seeming critical, mention your thoughts on the progress of the therapy.

Perhaps the therapist and modality are not a good fit for you. This sometimes happens. Advocate for yourself and consider switching therapists as you are investing time and money in your healing and the therapist and therapy should be effective.

Finding the right therapist is a bit like finding a partner. The process is multi-factorial and can include gender, age, communication style, preferred modality, and even a sense of humor and optimism. You are looking for the right fit for your therapy. It may take several therapists before you discover the right fit.

Chapter Activity: Writing about my daily expressions of admiration, appreciation, and affection for others today:

Date: _____

Begin each day by celebrating the best in yourself, others, and the world. Rather than see yourself in a societal rat race, see the beauty around you. In this activity, express your admiration, appreciation, and affection for others during the day. Rather than look for people's defects, seek out their strengths. Remember that your perceptions control your reality.

Compliment three people each day. Compliments make other people feel good. They also make others want to be around you. People love to be around positive people, and they will be more likely to listen to your ideas. You will feel better because of the positive impact you have on others. Make your compliments honest and kind.

Specific examples of how you express admiration, appreciation, and affection to others with whom and what:

1. _____

2. _____

3. _____

Specific compliments to others during the day with whom and what: _____

Chapter 6

Journaling

Pray, hope, and do not worry. Worry is useless. Our Merciful Lord will listen to your prayers.

Padre Pio

Benefits

Approach journaling prayerfully because it provides opportunities to put your worries associated with depression into writing. In doing this, you can consider writing about solutions through the gifts of the Holy Spirit.

Even if you begin with just five minutes at the end of the day, take the time to journal. Get those thoughts and feelings out of your head and down on paper or in a computer file. As you write about your journey to mental wellness, the world can seem more understandable, and the benefits of journaling are many.

Your journal writing helps you express feelings like depression, anxiety, joy, or love. In addition, you can describe how you are evolving as a person. By keeping a journal, you acknowledge and increase control of your feelings and improve your mental health.

Other benefits of journaling are thinking and writing about your present and future. As you look at today and tomorrow, journaling also provides opportunities to set goals. Once you commit your goals to paper or a computer file, they become more real.

With journaling, you can think about your short- and long-term ambitions and dreams. These can include your:

- Spiritual/religious goals. Ex. attending Mass and the holy days of obligation; prayer; reading the Bible, devotionals, or other spiritual writings
- Family goals. Ex. spending more quality time with your spouse or significant other, dining together, expressing gratitude to and for your family members
- Physical health goals. Ex. weight loss, exercise, medicine compliance
- Employment goals. Ex. being thankful for employment, taking a continuing education course in your field to improve job performance, seeking a promotion, further developing your employment skills
- Educational and school goals. Ex. attending school for a high school diploma or college degree, taking non-credit courses in your field of interest, pursuing a certificate in a trade, listening to Ted talks to improve work skills
- Intellectual and creative goals. Ex. reading about great men and women in American history, studying a language new to you, writing poetry or short stories
- Social interaction goals. Ex. joining a civic organization like Habitat for Humanity, the Rotary, a neighborhood association, or a faith-based community

Writing about your goals on paper or a computer screen makes them existent, authentic, and defined. Short and long-term goals supply tangible blueprints for your future. Just as a house is built with a blueprint, so can your life and destiny be planned with words. Journaling is also an opportunity for sincere self-exploration.

Significant benefits of journaling include cultivating mindfulness and living in the present, naming and writing about your feelings, enhancing your written communication skills, and increasing your self-confidence.

Journaling can bring you into a state of mindfulness, the present, by quieting your mental chatter and managing the complex feelings you may have, including your depression.

Journaling can also awaken joy within you. Fears and anxieties about your future fade in the present moment. Journaling can increase awareness of your thoughts, feelings, and past experiences. This state brings your sometimes-drifting mind into focus, from passivity to actively engaging with your ideas.

Naming and writing about your feelings. Journaling provides you with opportunities to name your feelings. You can be specific. For example, are you feeling depressed, stressed, content, or grateful? Naming these feelings enhances your emotional intelligence, which is the ability to perceive and manage your emotions. This action leads to understanding the feelings of others. Journaling is a means of increasing self-awareness.

Increasing self-discipline. Setting time aside to write, whether in the morning or evening, is an act of discipline. Like a muscle, the more you exercise it, the stronger it becomes. Moreover, habits that form in one area of your life- like scheduled writing times- tend to spread, such as keeping your desk tidy and closet organized.

Enhancing communication skills. Journaling forces you to think. Putting words on paper or at the keyboard increases your articulation, and the increased articulation in your writing spreads to how you think and talk with others. When you can put words on paper clearly, it becomes easier to do so in your speaking. This translates to being more effective and expressive in verbal communication.

Emotional healing. Journaling is a path to recovery. The healing can lead to stress reduction. When you write about a particularly joyful experience, you have an emotional release that diminishes your depression, anxiety, and stress. Journal writing improves your mood and boosts your well-being. Also, it can lead to more restful sleep.

Savor your past and present. Writing gives you opportunities to savor your past positive experiences. This savoring boosts your mood, fosters positive feelings, and increases your well-being. Think about a happy occasion, a wise decision you made, and ways you helped others. Think and write about how you are having a joy-filled day today.

With your journaling, find pleasure in your accomplishments, good fortune, and blessings. Be specific as you write. Think and write about the character strengths that helped you. You are making use of the gratitude character strength. When you savor, you spend time thinking and writing about your positive experiences.

What you think about is a choice. Choose to remember the good times regardless of childhood, adolescence, or recent problems. Do not concern yourself with your failures and disappointments but write about your successes and the good times you had. When good things happen to you now, like a promotion or an award, give yourself credit and acknowledge that you were responsible for bringing it about. Choose to look at your life through a lens of accomplishments and good times. It is your choice.

Journal about the wonder of people, places, and things. Savor the beauty of the seasons of the year. Watch the flowers and trees bloom in the spring. And write about this beauty in your journal. Marvel at the talents of athletes on a basketball court or soccer field. Marvel at dance, music, and art productions and appreciate the skills of those who create them. These are all great topics to journal about, leading to boosts in mood and well-being.

Journaling requires you to slow down. It leads to a conscious effort to be more mindful of what you are doing in the present and what is happening around you. Even in brief moments, you can be more attentive and engage in greater intention with your writing. You feel calmer and more in the present. Slowing down and being present in your writing helps you become more aware of what is happening to you and what you are doing.

Enhancing self-confidence. We all have memories of bitter disappointments, emotional hurts, and even trauma with our parents, children, friends, employers, or strangers. We are quick to recall them. Regardless of these hurts, we are also filled with memories of good times and moments of joy. Do not let these negative recollections bring you down.

Enhancing self-confidence requires a lens of joy for a mood boost. Your destiny in journaling can be a new way of seeing things around you. Rather than look at the past with its hurts through a sad lens, look at your history through the lens of happiness, appreciation, and joy. There is a choice in the lens you use.

Take a moment to think about the joy-filled moments in your life. Think about the kindness of people around you, someone who loved you dearly, a role model in your youth, or joy experienced in a beautiful place and time. Think about times you were filled with happiness and pride. Journal about these positive experiences, which will lead to mood boosts.

Journaling reaffirms your abilities when self-doubt appears. More importantly, it triggers the release of endorphins, which not only relieve pain but also enhance the healing process and creates a feeling of well-being. This release of endorphins heightens your self-confidence and mood, and journal reflections can become a catalog of personal achievements that you regularly go back to and reconsider.

Five Minutes A Day

Try to complete at least five minutes of journaling a day. This time can help you reduce your depression. Journaling enables you to prioritize problems, fears, and concerns. It gives you opportunities for positive self-talk and identifying and dismissing negative thoughts.

Journaling also helps you to write about any difficult current life experiences that are contributing to your depression. This writing can help you plan solutions to resolve them. Putting these solutions on paper or the computer screen leads to concretizing them and to act.

Suggestions for Journaling

Make it easy to journal. Keep a pen and notebook handy to jot down your thoughts. Researchers report that journaling is more effective with handwriting on paper. However, you can also journal at the keyboard or with an app on your cell phone.

Write whatever feels right. Your journal does not need to follow any structure or format. There are no rules for journaling; it is your private place to write about whatever you wish. Let the words flow freely without fussing. Do not worry about spelling or grammar mistakes.

You do not have to share your journal content with anyone. However, if you want to share some of your thoughts with your therapist, a loved one, or a trusted friend, you may read aloud or show them parts of your journal for discussion.

Keeping a journal helps you to establish order when your world seems chaotic. It enables you to get to know yourself by revealing your innermost fears, thoughts, and feelings. Look at your writing time as a personal relaxation time when you can relax, wind down, and be honest. Write in a relaxing and soothing place—near a window with natural light. Enjoy hot or iced coffee or tea.

Daily routines are vital in keeping emotional balance and a good mood. Make journaling a part of your daily routine. It is time to invest in yourself and affirm that you are thinking about and doing something good to reduce and even end your depression.

Pursue your authentic self in writing. Write with rigorous honesty about yourself but in a positive fashion. Try to limit negative words about yourself in your writing. Write about your moving on from resentments in your heart to forgiveness. Ideally, you have forgiven those who have hurt you. Christ makes it clear in the gospels that we must forgive others to be forgiven. We, as Catholics, must forgive the sins of others for God to forgive us.

Rigorous honesty in your journaling is demanding work and takes courage. It takes strength to consider behavioral changes that will lead to improved mental health. Be honest with the people in your life and acknowledge the truth of who you are. Date all your journal entries.

The journal can be an inexpensive spiral notebook, a simple composition book, or an ornate gilded monogrammed leather-bound volume. Handwrite or use a cheap Bic pen or handsome Montblanc Peggy writing instrument. You may also journal by authoring email messages to yourself or creating files or a journal folder on your desktop.

Therapeutic Rewards and Journal Organization

Therapeutic rewards from journaling include helping you track your progress with healing from depression and it records what you learn, think, and do as you grow stronger and feel better. Journal organizing techniques include:

Captured happy moments. Describe positive emotional experiences from your memory. These can include cherished memories when you were your best self and felt loved and cherished. They can be times when you were recognized for your accomplishments or kindness. As you allow your mind to drift, choose to focus on the happy moments.

Bullet lists. Write several related items in bullet lists to help prioritize and organize. Lists can include, for example, the thinking and behavioral tools you are developing from reading this book and others and the specific actions you plan to complete.

Letters of appreciation. Write letters to thank people who have helped you in your life because we all stand on the shoulders of those who have loved, guided, and supported us. Writing letters can also tell people about things you wish you had said or done.

Has a teacher helped you with life-changing career guidance? Has a friend or family member helped you with significant transitions in your life? Has a priest helped you by providing grief counseling after the death and burial of a loved one? These letters may or may not be sent. You can share these letters in therapy. Use the lens of gratitude.

Dialogue and scriptwriting. Write nontraditionally. Create both sides to a conversation between yourself and another person. The person can be your mother, a dear friend, a deceased teacher, a favorite priest, or a stranger. The dialogue can focus on a particular event or a meaningful time in your life. Your journaling can be in the form of scriptwriting.

For those interested in script writing with your journaling, visit Nashville Film Institute's (NFI) "Script Writing: Everything you Need to Know" on the internet featuring suggestions from Quinton Tarantino with online classes and resources.

Doodles and drawings. You may have artistic talent. If you find yourself doodling more than writing in your journal, commit to a journal of doodles and graphics. You are the author. If you prefer doodles and drawings to phrases and writing narratives, then so be it.

Random writing prompts. You can respond to short phrases or words you overhear in conversations, in a chat with friends, things heard in meetings, or even lyrics from your favorite song. Emphasize your best self. Pursue hope.

Settings for Journaling

Find a quiet place at home, a park, or a coffee shop for journaling. This environment ideally has elements that relax you. Listen to your favorite music or enjoy a hot or cold drink. Avoid loud, distracting, crowded, or cluttered places. A calm environment helps you to focus and associate good feelings with journal writing.

Journal writing sessions can start with simple deep breathing exercises. Then, after journal writing, you may do mild stretching. Consider listening to calming music or talking to a friend after you journal.

Chapter Activity: Journal Prompt Completions

Following is a list of journal prompts to write about. Take your time with them. Ponder and write about each prompt thoughtfully. Date your work.

1. How do I feel today?

   _____

2. What am I grateful for today?

   _____

3. If in therapy, what is my assessment of the time and money

   spent and how do I feel about it?

   _____

4. How can I improve my relationships with family members,

   friends, and acquaintances?

   _____

5. How can I improve my prayer life?

   _____

6. How can I better contribute my skills and talents to my

   Catholic Church?

   _____

Chapter 7

Embrace a Heightened Quality of Life

Loving God, you are always near those who have a mental illness.
Lift our burdens, calm our anxiety, and quiet our fears. Surround
us with your healing presence.

Our Lady of Lourdes

Introduction

Healing Your Depression: A Catholic Perspective, 2nd Ed., has
suggested prayer without ceasing, church attendance, and enhanced
thought processes and routines to end your depression. Each activity
contributes to your wellbeing.

During the reading and over time, you have become a practicing
Catholic adhering to the five precepts of the Catholic Church
outlined by Father Worku Gebre in the Foreword and found in *The
Catechism of the Catholic Church.* And the church has become your
cherished second home.

Personal relationships have become a priority. More important
than work, you are investing more energy and time in your family

members and friends. You are feeling more connected with others and are thankful for your small circle of friends who care about you. The relationships with both parents and children are improving. You are better able to live, love, and work in society.

Perhaps you are taking better care of your physical health by seeing a medical provider regularly and taking medicines for chronic ailments. For diabetic hypertensives, your sugar levels and blood pressure are under control. Your dietary habits have improved. You are exercising regularly and have lost weight.

You have reduced or cut your vape, cigarette, or chewing tobacco use. You are no longer abusing prescription or recreational drugs if this was a problem. You have ended or at least reduced your alcohol intake. You liquor store ABC visits are fewer and your supermarket shopping baskets are no longer filled with wine bottles

You may have joined a 12-step program if alcohol, drug, or food addiction was a problem. Your higher power in the program is God or your personal relationship with Jesus Christ comforts you. You rely more heavily on the voice and gifts of the Holy Spirit in addiction recovery.

You follow new sleep hygiene practices. The quality and length of your sleep each night have both improved. You awaken clear-headed, refreshed, and hopeful from a decent night's sleep. If you have been diagnosed with obstructive sleep apnea, you are now using your C-pap or bi-pap machine regularly for more restful sleep.

You are now familiar with the VIA Character Institute on its website. You know about its surveys, books, and online positive psychology classes. You completed the free survey to learn about your signature character strengths and you periodically review the report as it boosts your mood.

You share your five signature character strengths with family members and close friends. You think about how you share these character strengths daily and recognize the character strengths demonstrated in others. You are knowledgeable about positive psychology; you refer to the PERMA Model daily.

After some soul searching, you have entered into a therapeutic relationship with a licensed mental health provider. After a careful search, you now see a talk therapist who is a good fit for you, and you find therapy helpful. The therapist's modality is helping, and you sense that you are getting better.

You are more hopeful and comfortable with yourself and life due to your work inside and outside the therapy sessions. You keep notes of your sessions and the homework for your therapy sessions has been both revealing and uplifting, and you occasionally review the completed written assignments. You have become a wiser consumer of mental health services.

If you are seeing a psychiatrist or psychiatric nurse practitioner, you may be prescribed a psychotropic medicine or a medicine cocktail for your clinical depression diagnosis. The prescribed medication is only temporary and supplements your weekly or bi-weekly talk therapy sessions.

You are now a more well-informed consumer of your prescribed psychotropics. You have studied them and are now familiar with their classifications such as the SSRIs, SNRIs, NMDs, the hypnotics, anxiolytics, and others, and their reported benefits to your brain chemistry. You are mindful of the side effects and discuss them with your prescriber. If you have chosen to stop the medicine, you have discussed medicine termination with the prescriber to avoid serious medical consequences.

Over time, your depression is lifted. You have moments of joy and serenity. You are no longer preoccupied with the past or apprehensive about the future. You do not ruminate over your past hurtful actions. You enjoy the present and are hopeful about the future.

You are more comfortable with your body. With some weight loss, your blood chemistries have improved and you feel more attractive.

Perhaps you now limit your time on the social media platforms. While hundreds of millions of Americans use Instagram, YouTube, Facebook, Twitter, TikTok, Pinterest, or Snapchat daily, you are now less enthusiastic about your time and connections with others on the platforms. Maybe you realize that your hours daily on the platforms are wasteful and even counterproductive.

If you have adolescent children, your communication with them has improved. You frequently warn them of the sexual predators on Facebook, the many chatrooms, and other platforms filled with fake people, traffickers, and predators.

Quality-of-Life Lens

A way to view your changing world and healing is by using your Quality-of-Life Lens. This lens includes different domains including the physical, psychological, social, environmental, independence, and spiritual and religious domains.

The domains influence how you think, act, and live. These domains govern how you spend your time and with whom and affect your inner and external life and the relationships you have with yourself and others. As you review the quality-of-life domains, consider those improvements you have made- or plan to make- on your path of healing to improved well-being.

Physical Domain

You understand the connection between physical and mental wellness. You are under the care of a licensed medical professional for your ailments and general health. Your physical health has improved, and you are managing your chronic diseases like hypertension, diabetes, or obesity more effectively. You have greater energy with improved physical fitness, and the fatigue has lifted. You are more active and sleep better.

Psychological Domain

You have more positive feelings about yourself and life. Your self-esteem has improved. You are more hopeful about tomorrow. Those painful feelings accompanying the negative mind chatter are reduced. Your depression and anxiety are diminished.

Social Domain

Relationships with your spouse or partner, family members, friends, and colleagues have improved. You are rigorously honest and authentic about yourself with others. You have learned that it feels good to be honest and you are more genuine in your communications with family and friends. Self-condemning mental chatter has subsided and has been replaced by more accepting self-talk.

You have found those around you who provide positive social support. You no longer feel alone or disconnected from others. You can quickly name, with gratitude, a handful of people in your life with whom you feel connected.

Environmental Domain

Issues with income, money, monthly budgeting, and work have improved. You have learned to live within your budget and enjoy your work more. You are learning skills for improved work performance. You have a new hobby or are taking an interesting online class.

You may have changed your physical environment with a relocation to another house or apartment, town, state, or nation. You live in a place you can afford, and the location has your desired amenities. For some, it may be a relocation to a large and densely populated city in northeastern United States. For others, it may be settling in a sleepy small town or hamlet in the deep south.

With a sense of adventure, perhaps you have joined the ten million American citizens, excluding military personnel, living in over one hundred countries in 2023 according to the U.S. State Department in Washington, DC, and the Association of Americans, Residents Overseas (AARO) based in Paris, France. These millions of Americans reside for brief and extended residencies in, for example, Canada, Australia, Singapore, Great Britain, and Spain. Medical and dental care quality overseas often equals or exceeds that found in the United States and at reduced costs with greatly increased accessibility.

Thousands live in Ecuador, the Philippines, and Thailand, where the cost of living is considerably less for a decent and comfortable quality of life. Those who teach English as a second language (ESL), or are digital nomads enjoy the excitement and cultural challenges of overseas life.

There are also thousands of truly blessed Americans who currently dedicate their lives to volunteering when natural disasters occur, for example, in Indonesia, Mexico, or Pakistan. You find them at the sites of earthquakes, hurricanes, typhoons, and floods. These volunteers often learn that they have little time to be depressed because they live a life engaged in altruistic and meaningful work.

Independence Domain

You are busy living life with all that it entails. You do not have substance abuse problems. You are not abusing or relying on alcohol, prescription or recreational drugs, or tobacco products. These changes have resulted in improving your mental and physical health.

You may have joined one of the 12-step programs to aid you with your addictions including food. You have emersed yourself with daily or weekly meetings, daily readings, and enjoy new friendships in the mutual-support-group culture.

Your abilities at work have heightened. You see more meaning in your work and your work performance has improved. You approach your employment more as a profession and not simply a job to pay the bills. Whether you are serving fast food, manufacturing widgets, teaching a university class, or doing cardiothoracic surgery, you are grateful to be gainfully employed and productive.

Spiritual and Religious Domain

Ideally, you have become more active in your Catholic Church community. Your faith community supplies opportunities for spiritual, prayer, and social activities. You have become more involved in your prayer life, attend Mass regularly, and receive the Sacraments of Reconciliation and the Eucharist.

You now say prayers of thanksgiving daily. Perhaps one of your signature character strengths is now "gratitude" and your life is filled with thankfulness. You ask for guidance from Jesus. You rely upon the gifts of the Holy Spirit. You have learned that you are never alone.

Chapters Review

Review the chapters of *Healing Your Depression: A Catholic Perspective, 2nd Ed.* What topics are now more relevant and meaningful to you? Which chapter did you read a second time? Did you write, fill in any of the lines, or doodle in the book? If so, read the entries again. Did you underline or highlight specific passages in the book? As you re-read, did you find other passages that are now meaningful to you? Was there anything in this book that spoke directly to you about relief from depression and your journey to well-being?

Have you been journaling? If so, take out your journal and review the entries from the beginning. Have you seen changes in your attitudes? Have your attitudes about yourself and others changed? Have you written about the depth and periods of depression diminishing? What changes in behavior have you recorded in your journal?

Spend time congratulating yourself on the changes you have orchestrated in your life. You are, like everyone else, a work in progress. Your life is far from perfect, but it has improved. You say to yourself, "I am okay. Life is good. I am blessed."

Each of us defines the quality of our lives differently. Regardless of your family or genetic background, educational background, socioeconomic status at birth, geographic residence, or financial resources, you are influenced by the quality-of-life domains. How did your quality of your life change among the six domains? Was one domain weightier than another?

About Happiness

With your depression reduced or eliminated and your spiritual and physical health improving, discussing the concept of happiness is reasonable and realistic.

St. Augustine and St. Thomas Aquinas wrote about human desire and the need for happiness. They asserted that happiness includes both inner (soul/mind) and outer (physical) goods. They affirmed that the pursuit of happiness is important and necessary for a worthwhile human life.

Most importantly, these saints asserted that happiness of soul and body can be found in God- the Father, the Son, and Holy Spirit. If we seek to delight in God, to love Him above all things, and to love others and the self for God's sake, then we can know true and lasting happiness. Happiness is measured globally.

The nations of Denmark, Finland, and Switzerland continue to lead the world in the global happiness and well-being scales. These countries have a nationwide commitment to all for quality free education, free health care for all, food abundance, and communal support and kindness in their societies. These countries have little violent crime, sexual or other physical violence, obesity, or addiction. For example, while the United States mourns the nearly weekly school gun shootings in 2023, the last school shooting in Denmark was in 1994.

The "Nation Master" website provides reliable global comparative statistics on crime, economic variables, employment, education duration and spending, and divorce rates. To learn more about global happiness, visit the World Population Review website on the internet. The governments of Denmark, Finland, and Switzerland consider the pursuit of happiness among all residents as a priority.

The United States continues to drop on the global happiness scale. At nineteenth in 2021, it trails behind counties like Germany, Canada, Costa Rico, and the Czech Republic. One might wonder how and why happiness is diminishing for most people in American society.

Researchers suggest that the national drop in happiness results from changes in our lifestyles. Many residents are challenged by economic hardship and the federal government reports that one in five children in 2023 lives in a home with food insecurity.

Access to quality, affordable health care is key to happiness, healthier lives, economic security, and peace of mind. Even with the Affordable Care Act plan efforts and Medicaid, in 2022, there were twenty-six million Americans without any form of health insurance. Being uninsured limits access to even the most basic medical care and only emergency pain-related dental care.

Five hundred seventy thousand persons were awarded Social Security Disability benefits in 2021 alone indicating severe health and work challenges. Forty-one million persons nationally were receiving Supplemental Nutrition Assistance Program (food stamps, ETB) in 2022 and the number grows.

The medical, dental, and prescription costs are reported to be excessive in 2023 and prohibitive costs limit basic care for those with medical and dental problems. Barriers include the expense of seeing a clinician and the shortage of primary care medical providers who accept all forms on health insurance including Medicaid. Some people must choose between prescribed medicines purchase and meals.

According to the Healthline and the U.S. Health and Human Services websites, only ninety-three percent of primary care providers accept Medicare in 2023. Only seventy percent are now accepting new Medicare patients and this number is dropping annually. The reason for Medicare denial is reduced reimbursement rates to the medical providers. This is a cause for concern to older Americans.

"Medical gaslighting," has also become a more severe problem in post-pandemic America. It is a term used to describe medical providers who deny or dismiss a patient's perceived symptoms and illness. For example, they may tell their patients- more often women and those of color- that they are not really sick or blame a patient's symptoms on "psychological factors" which leads to inadequate medical care and increased stress for the patient who is not heard. This rare medical provider downplays the symptoms, fails to engage in follow-up questions, does not record the complaint in the patient's medical record, and ignores the patient's medical complaints. The internet provides information on medical gaslighting and the patient's effective solutions to the problem.

Many researchers identify the recent dip in happiness to the invention of smartphones which have replaced human interpersonal communications. Other researchers suggest that it is the nation's time-consuming enthusiasm for social platform use like Twitter, TikTok, and Instagram. Still, others blame Facebook because it is reported to lead to Facebook addiction and Facebook envy.

Researchers at the Massachusetts Institute of Technology (MIT) in Cambridge blame the current preoccupation with economic growth and profits among businesses. There is little concern for environmental pollution, social support of the disenfranchised, and visceral political polarization leading to diminished happiness. There is also a decline in the middle class according to the Pew Research Center.

For detailed information about the decline of America's middle class, visit the Pew Research Center website. Read the recent reports on the shrinking middle class and its ramifications on the quality of life in America.

Happiness Solutions

Challenge the diminished societal happiness trends. There are solutions for you to increase happiness at the personal level. Martin Seligman's groundbreaking book, *Authentic Happiness*, and his promotion of positive psychology discusses happiness at a level over which each one of us has control. We have personal control over our levels of happiness.

His theory of authentic happiness is that happiness can be examined by looking at three elements. These elements are:

- Experiencing positive emotions
- Engaging with others in positive ways
- Finding meaning in our actions

Seligman describes recognizing and using your twenty-four-character strengths. These character strengths, from the VIA Institute on Character, are listed and described in Chapter 3 of this book. This effort meshes with your application of the PERMA Model. The model and its five elements were also previously discussed in that chapter.

Researchers who study happiness suggest that it occurs by using a set of habits. Regardless of socioeconomic, physical health status, or disposable income, the habits of happy people include:

- Building or enhancing warm relationships with family members, friends, co-workers, and others
- Performing daily random acts of kindness to others
- Focusing on your physical well-being with proper nutrition, exercise, exposure to natural light, weight maintenance, and sleep

- Experiencing "flow" by doing the things you deeply appreciate, like playing sports, writing, creating art or music, or travel

- Using your signature character strengths and seeing these character strengths in others
- Finding meaning in life through your activities and relationships
- Having a positive mindset which includes gratitude, savoring life's activities, and experiencing feelings of hope.

You have learned that healing from your depression is entirely possible. And so, too, is experiencing happiness. According to Pope Francis, those who believe in God are blessed; they are happy. He says that happiness is not in having something or becoming someone special. Wealth and titles are not predictors of happiness. "True happiness is being with the Lord and loving and caring for ourselves, our families, Catholic Church families, and society."

Our Pope Francis also says that the ingredients for a happy life are found in the beatitudes. In his recent papal writings on happiness, he states, "Blessed are the humble who make room for God, who can weep for others and for their own mistakes, fight for justice, and are merciful to all."

He goes on to say, "Blessed are those who safeguard the purity of heart, always work for peace, do not hate and, even when suffering, respond to malice with love."

Chapter Activity: Write about my life's improvements using a quality-of-life lens.

Date: _____

List ways that the quality of my life has improved. List the physical, mental, and behavioral changes associated with the domains.

1. _____

2. _____

3. _____

Chapter Activity: How I can better embrace each of the habits of a happy person.

Date: _____

Habit/Action

1. _____

2. _____

3. _____

Life Synopsis of the Author

Born in NYC * Raised on Long Island * SUNY- Cortland State College (B.S.Ed.), the University of North Carolina at Chapel Hill (MPH), Southern Illinois University at Carbondale (Ph.D.) * Peace Corps Volunteer, W.H.O. Smallpox Eradication Program, Ethiopia * Lt, U.S. Marine Corps * Clinic Administrator, NC and NY * Associate Professor, Health Care Administration, Western Kentucky University, James Madison University (retired) * Volunteer Associate Professor of Public Health, Haramaya and Gondar Universities, Ethiopia * Instructor, Zhengzhou Foreign Language School, Henan Province, China * Instructor, English Rhetoric, University of North Ecuador, Ibarra * Writing Consultant, Eastern Mennonite University, Virginia

Recent Publications

The author's recent publications are available on Amazon.com in paperback and Kindle formats.

- *Healing You Depression: A Catholic Perspective (2022).* Foreword by Rev. Fr. Worku Yohannes Gebre
- *Confessional Poems and Vignettes* [T.R. Syre as author]
- *Healing Your Addictions: Guide to Outpatient and Residential Treatment.* Foreword by James L. Krag, MD
- *Ethiopia's Mothers and Children: Public Health Research in 2012*
- *Write a Great Thesis! Guidebook for International Students Studying in the United States* co-authored by Tom Syre, Jr.
- *The Action Research Project Paper: A Primer for Undergraduate and Graduate Students*

Maternal-child health, third-world infectious diseases, substance abuse, and higher education research papers and books published prior to 2018 are found by browsing Google Scholar and ResearachGate.net.

Prayer to St. Dymphna, Patron Saint for Mental Wellness

Good Saint Dymphna, great wonderworker in every affliction of mind, I humbly implore your powerful intercession with Jesus through Mary, the health of the sick, in my present need of healing from depression. Saint Dymphna, martyr of purity, patroness of those who suffer from nervous and mental afflictions, beloved child of Jesus and Mary, pray to them for me and obtain my request.

Amen.

Index

Active Minds, 115

Addictions, healing your, 81

Adult Children of Alcoholics (ACoA), 44

Al-Anon, 44

Alcohol and drugs, 42

Antidepressants, antianxiety medicines, 60, 122, 124

Application, PERMA Model, 41, 161, 190

Appointment, your first with a therapist, 129, 131

Behavioral change, 67,142, 175

Budgeting, 19, 53

Catholic Mental Health Ministries, 24

Catholic Suicides, 24

Character strengths, 49, 101, 104

Cognitive Behavioral therapy (CBT), 45, 129,139

College campus counseling centers, 114

College campus religious organizations, 118

Community Services Boards (CSB), 45, 110

Couples and family therapy, 138, 143

Duckworth, Angela, 50, 130, 138

Diet, healthier, 91

Drug addiction treatment, 81

DSM-5, 126, 136, 140, 151

Emotions Anonymous (EA), 160

Examination, physical, 11, 69, 75

Exercise, 26, 88

Facebook, 20, 22

Federally qualified community health centers, 73

Financial planning, 52

Firearms, 25

Food pantries, 86

Gaslighting, medical, 189

Golden rule adherence, 41, 97 98

Gratitude, 47, 103, 133, 164

Happiness, about, 105, 186, 190

High-intensity drinking, 43

Holistic therapy, 145

Holy Spirit, 2, 37, 63, 67,110, 155,165, 180, 185

Hotlines, suicide, 23, 26

Homework in therapy, 34, 36, 129, 132. 181

Hospitalization, psychiatric, 12, 158

Journaling benefits, 169, 172

Lenses, application of, 12, 13, 49,96,148, 150

Lifestyle, 11,19,29,30, 65, 67, 68

Marijuana and recreation drugs, 78

Medications, 10, 11, 30, 60, 70,77, 112, 123, 125

Meditation, 57

Mental exercises, 162

Mindfulness, 56, 58, 146, 150

Minimalism, 18

Motivational enhancement therapy, 138, 141

Newscast viewing, 38

New life's resolutions, 69

Obesity, 27

Overeaters Anonymous (OA), 31

PERMA Model, 2, 41, 118, 152, 153, 161, 166, 181

Physical health, 41

Physical examination, 69, 75

Physical exercise, 26

Pope Francis, 3, 5, 14, 15, 18, 97, 191

Popular therapeutic modalities, 135, 166

Positive psychology modality, 13, 30, 138, 147

Positive psychology in schools, 115

Positive psychology center, 105

Post-traumatic growth, 48, 143

Psychiatric nurse practitioners, 112, 127, 136, 181

Psychiatrists, 2, 26,112, 122, 123, 124, 126, 127

Quality of life lenses, 182, 191

Rasid, Tayyab, 143

Recovering couples anonymous (RCA), 145

Relationships, 3, 8, 31, 37, 48, 59, 63, 95,102, 105

Record keeping, 132

Registered dietician (R.D.), 30, 92, 146

Resilience, 49, 51, 90, 161

Search methods, therapist, 109, 112

Self-advocacy, 137

Settings for journaling, 177

Shoener, Deacon Ed, 24

Seligman, Martin, 149, 130,138, 143, 149, 152, 190

Sleep, 8, 46, 59, 70, 83, 87, 92, 118, 172, 180, 183, 190

Social connections, 21, 59, 60

Sood, Amit, 50

Social media, 20, 22, 23, 26, 76, 182

St. Dymphna, Patron Saint, mental wellness, 197

Stress and its management, 86

Suicide, 5, 9, 23,24,25, 33,114, 157,158

Teletherapy, 119

Therapist search methods, 109, 132

Therapy, things to ask about; don't be shy, 129

Tobacco products, 82, 180, 185

Transtheoretical Model, 67

Trauma inventories, 49

U.S. Veterans Affairs Administration, 49, 80

VIA Institute on Character, 12, 101, 104, 130, 163, 180, 190

Virtues and character strengths, 101, 105

Woititz, Janet, 4

Oremus

Made in the USA
Middletown, DE
05 March 2023

26061602R00116